Dedicated to Jesse Adoquei, Aunty Adjokor
and Julian Casablancas.

Acknowledgment

My more than 30 years of professional experience would not have mattered had I not been challenged by my talented and unique students with their insatiable appetite to learn. Since I started my career at the age of 14, I've met nothing but the most challenging, experienced and knowledgeable artists with questions that have consistently kept me on my toes. For this, I would like to recognize and acknowledge the National Academy School of Fine Arts, the Art Students League, Lyme Academy and The New York Academy of Figurative Arts for employing me at a time when the language was foreign, the culture very different and new. Writing this book has been the biggest and most enjoyable challenge that I have encountered.
Writing this book has been a demanding venture. Modern ideas and commercialization has made a scientific subject of how to acquire technical skills very abstract. Reasoning to make clear and differentiate what is Art and what is the Science of art made the task complex but interesting. I'd like to recognize and acknowledge the valuable editing experience of my great and kind editor Martha Crow. Martha made this book possible. Without her, I would have given up. In particular, I would like to thank Nancy Little and Gail Buxton for their willingness to help proof read the book. Special thanks to Jennifer King for all her editing help over the years.
I would like to thank Marie-France Siegler of Chateau de Pecany who provided me with friendship and the relaxing atmosphere of the French countryside, and Mr. Richard Stone and Tom Shea for all they have done for me. Also thanks to Nancy Wolff, Douglas Eisenberg and Matthew J. Simon and my contemporary artists friends Jeanette Christjansen, Usha Sharma, Karen Haider, Brad Kaden and Oldrich Teply. Thank you all for everything. Thank you for being my friend. I believe that, although this book is not perfect, it is my contribution to improving the learning habits of today's talents. I hope you share this opinion. Lastly, I would like to thank the United States for giving me the greatest opportunities, all the platforms and freedom.

HOW TO USE THIS BOOK.

How Successful Artists Study has 18 chapters with over 90 images; both chapters and images are not in a special sequence. Unless otherwise stated, all images are for enjoyment. The book is put together this way for the reader to have freedom to start from whichever chapter he desires and browse through the pages to enjoy images.

The book is filled with rich colorful reproductions of masterpieces by artists with different styles and different vision, it is a catalog of Masterpieces by American, French, German and Spanish Masters, like John Singer Sargent, Frank Duveneck, Henry Fantin Latour and Joaquin Sorolla; Old Masters like Anthony Van Dyke, Lucas Cranach and many contemporary artists; Sigmund Abeles, Mary Beth Mckenzie, Lisa Dinhofer, Jeanette Christjansen, Usha Sharma, including works by the author.

CONTENTS

PREFACE

Conventional wisdom has it that those who paint cannot also teach or write, and that those who write or teach, cannot paint. There is a little truth to this paradigm because in recent times one chooses a very specific branch from the field of art and then specializes in that one area. It was not like this in the past—then the artist was the educator, the scholar, the creator, and the master of his workshop. In all, this conventional wisdom is a false paradigm; it is false because artists have written some of the best books or treatises on art. Giorgio Vasari, an Italian artist, wrote a well-known book on artists and techniques, for instance. Leonardo da Vinci wrote about his theories of art, as did Albrecht Dürer, Eugène Delacroix, and many more. These are books all professional artists are familiar with, and all these books were written by professional artists. In a real sense the paradigm is misleading if one considers the fact that only the practitioner who has been working in his field for a long time, and who therefore believes in it, knows it well enough to teach it. He alone should be the qualified expert on the subject. Such has been the case for all great books on particular subjects.

As the saying goes, a word to the wise is enough; sometimes a life can change or improve because of a single phrase of advice, a quote or a mantra. Sometimes a simple conversation or a book, an experience, even a feeling, can convert the listener or reader from an unproductive life to a progressive, successful one. Any of these sources of motivation can trigger the change that has long been waiting in the subconscious—it happens when the person who needs to change hears the quote, or reads the passage, or has an experience that triggers action. In some ways, all students have what it takes to turn their artistic abilities into the realization of their dreams. What is needed for things to happen is hidden until they search for it. They search and search for that trigger in hopes that the right way of learning will show up. Instead of waiting for the right ideas to show up, why not find them by asking the right questions? After all, that is what most successful people do—and that is the reason for this book. Within these pages the reader will find clues and pointers on how to pursue a life in art. Most of the clues will be in the form of questions or suggestions.

Often all that a student needs is simple logical advice, advice that makes a lot of sense to him, and then his views towards learning will be changed forever. This book is the embodiment of the quote, that a word to the wise is sufficient. The opinions, ideas, reasons, advice and questions are here for the student to consider in the hope that a sentence or a paragraph, a chapter or the whole book will help the student gain a realistic overview of the vocation of art, and to plan well before enrolling in an art school.

By no means do I claim that this book is for everybody. Or that it has answers for every problem the art students may have. The study of art is too complex for me to claim such a thing. I have concentrated on what I have learned from my own life's experiences—my more than thirty years of teaching experience, plus some surveys I have conducted of art students. A book like this is what is needed for today's art student—a book by a professional artist and educator. This book is intended to help bring awareness to the art student of the adventures most students face while learning to become artists, and to help safeguard the student during decision-making times.

My background makes this book unique. Coming from Africa, I have had to realize that I couldn't afford to slack off. As a result, I learned the effective way to approach the pursuit of art as a vocation, and it is this that inspires my book. My goal is to write a unique and new book for today's student—an ideal book in the form of a mentor in a book, full of ideas and advice that can only come from an artist with my diverse background. I have more than thirty years of teaching experience, training and helping artists. I also base the book on my experience of making a career in New York's art world. This book is intended for those who want to make sure their time at school is well spent. In writing this book, my goal has been to keep to a broad overview of the study of art, rather than a view based on one particular art tradition.

Figure 2 USHA SHARMA, *The Thinker, oil on canvas*

Figure 1 JEANETTE CHRISTJANSEN, *Three Qunices, oil on canvas*

Once the message is clear the artist does not have to technically over work the artwork. This painting illustrates the idea that a finished painting does not necessarily have to look like a Old Master painting. It is called "non finito" technique. It is a technique used a lot by Michelangelo Buonarrotti (1475-1564) during his matured years and was used by other great artists. Michelangelo argues that an artwork is finished when the message is conveyed.

INTRODUCTION

If all important and successful life journeys require good planning, then the artist's life is no exception.

I once asked one of the advanced students, a hard-working student, "How will you live on your art after school?"

He answered: "I don't know."
"What will you paint after school," I asked.
"I don't know," he replied.
"Which galleries will you show your work to?"
"I don't know."
"How will you support yourself?"

The common myth among students is that if they work very hard, success will automatically favor them. Yet we know from experience that the law of success only selects those who think right and do the right thing. He who can answer the above questions off the top of his head will be the student in control of his studies, his future and his career.

The field of traditional art education is very unique and very personal; because of this there aren't specific books written on how exactly one should approach the learning of art. Its uniqueness makes it difficult to have one theory that will suit all students; besides that it will require a teacher who practices art as a profession and who is at the same time an educator with versatile experience. Technical "how to" books are written mainly by professional artists, and books or essays on art education are often written by scholars who themselves are not artists. They have never been on the street, out there with their portfolios going from gallery to gallery, searching for someone to represent their artwork. And they have never worked in a painting studio in a traditional environment dealing with real life situations and experiences. The scholar with all his knowledge and the full-time professional artist, who survives by working as an artist, often have different views on how to approach art as a vocation; their advice will only be useful to an informed individual who already knows what he wants. These opposing viewpoints have made such a book impossible up to now. And it is this that has opened the door for me to put together a special book for today's student: a special book to make the contemporary student wise by learning how to acquire the right experience and knowledge while attending school. If you want to be a scholar or an historian and follow the steps of the scholar's path, then this book is not for you. This book is good for anyone willing to pursue art in the traditional sense, which means painting in a studio with a professional artist watching over your shoulders, providing advice and hands-on technical help.

All students have the potential to become as good as they envision themselves capable of becoming, but often the lack of constructive and objective advice from a professional artist makes their goal harder to achieve.

This book is suggestive and pragmatic, but it is not a recipe. It consists of ideas and insights that I have gathered over my thirty years as an artist and teacher, as well as through interviews and surveys I have conducted over the years, to help you, the reader, the new, talented artist, learn more in order to create with confidence after finishing school. I also want to help you, the student, learn to be more realistic and more logical in making decisions both during and also before your art education, so that you will have a clear plan to help you develop important practical skills that can guide you in finding your voice, your freedom and after school, your artistic success.

This book is meant to be a guide that empowers students, as they go through their art education, to proceed with ease and thereby encounter a no-frustration school.

I wrote this book because I believe it is helpful to have advice and guidance from a professional who has the knowledge and experience gained from having made the same decisions you will be making. This book will help you so you won't need to go through the whole experience again and again; you will get it right the first time.

CHALLENGES FACING TODAY'S STUDENT
(Food for Thought)

In our advanced society, where the cost of living is so high, how did studying art get to such a point, that a student can invest in high tuition and spend many years of his life learning how to make art, yet the trained artist needs more than artistic expertise to survive on his art? At school, there is no promise that the student will learn enough about his field to have the freedom to choose the style he wishes to use in order create well, nor is there a promise that he will learn what it takes to live and survive as a professional artist.

Whose fault is this? Who is responsible? It is no one's fault—the uniqueness of the field makes it impossible to have a predictable approach and to guarantee results. No one is responsible; the problem is caused by the very nature of art, the freedom it gives to the artist and the freedom of expression it allows students to approach art in the way they prefer. How did it get to a point that it is considered unnecessary to learn the basic rules of survival as an artist? Is it the fault of the naïve student, who didn't know how to prepare and appreciate and respect the field and didn't know what to expect from school before diving headfirst into art, or is it the fault of the artistic structure designed by scholars and dealers who do not live it (the field of art) or practice the true and realistic life of the artist, on the street and in real life.

I lived from the practice of my art in Africa, and in the United States, I have lived on my art since about two years after my arrival. All this was due to the advice I got as a student. My goal here is to share some experience and suggestions that can bring awareness to the student so that he or she can avoid being the victim of a fate that has produced frustration, lost dreams and unfulfilled ambitions. Let him rather enjoy the whole process of learning, and have confidence and courage that he too can take his educational experience and knowledge and build a profession, while still producing innovative works that will allow him to pursue his vision.

The artist in pursuit of total freedom, or self-identity, very early in his studies can naïvely forget what to demand from his learning environment, and what is the purpose of an art school, the sacrifice required of a student in order to acquire all the necessary knowledge schools and studios have to offer. Our modern world's enticing philosophical idea says that everything goes; this has

allowed the hardworking, ambitious and talented art student to forget the difference between a student and an artist. Because of this, the student's talent is no
longer challenged and tested so he can come to fully understand and know his
potential while a student, and how to use his abilities after school. The aim of
the discussions in this book is to enlighten the would-be artist on how to use
his student years for cultivating and crafting his talent, how to develop the correct attitude and views toward learning so that his potential and destiny are not
decided by outside forces that he has no control over. Without any of the realistic information or guidelines set forth in this book, the time and tuition spent in
school will be too costly.

The duty of the art student, who is paying tuition for years, is to learn how
to acquire the necessary skills to pursue art as a vocation, and to understand
and accept the worlds outside the parameters of the studio. Being aware of the
existence of the practical and realistic worlds outside gives the artist more control over how he will craft his art, his career and his future, and how he can follow his dreams and ambitions. On the other hand, the student who is unaware
and uninformed regarding important artistic and educational decisions puts
everything in the hands of luck to decide his future. This book is to inform the
student that artistic achievements come easily if the student plans well.

On the other hand, the naïve student who stays in his internal idealistic art
world while studying makes himself vulnerable, allowing society to eventually
rob him of his artistic freedom. The freedom to be creative yet productive and
useful to society and to sell his artwork in order to create and live as he wishes.

The number of years of freedom the student sacrifices at school to learn the
right way will depend on the individual student's ambitions, goals and dreams.
The grander his ambitions and dreams, the more contentedly the student will
endure his student days.

Throughout this book, one point I will continuously stress is, the student,
unaware of some common faults in making decisions in learning art, can create
unnecessary difficulties for himself during his student years. Why should it be
easy to learn the right way for some students with a certain kind of attitude and
approach and information, yet very difficult for other students? Why shouldn't
that knowledge that has helped a few students successfully learn the craft be
available to those students who unintentionally make all the wrong decisions
and choices? In the study of art too much emphasis is put on technique. Why
should a wrong approach innocently cost a student so much of his life's invest-

ment? Perhaps during the period of studying the student never had the opportunity to be guided in the right way. Why should luck be the sole determination of an innocent student's future? How can the innocent student know what the right approach or that certain way is, if the knowledge is not available? Perhaps, on the one hand, the study of art is approached too abstractly in modern times and, on the other hand, because of art's uniqueness, answers regarding the questions of art allow too much freedom to the innocent student.

Figure 3

SAMUEL ADOQUEI,
*Legacy of Dr. Martin
Luther King,
unfinished*

Figure 4 SAMUEL ADOQUEI, *Ed Leibston*

CHAPTER ⋖O1⋗

HOW MUCH TALENT
DOES THE STUDENT NEED?

If you think you need talent to become an artist, you are wrong. If you think you need special talent to become a good artist, you are still wrong. You don't need to be born with an amazing talent to become a genius in the arts.

Nature does not create artists, dentists, soldiers, or computer geeks. The creator created humans with versatile coconuts who can rise to the occasion if the desire to do so is there. The heart and the mind can develop such a strong will that the only impossible things are those scientifically and humanly impossible to man. What we end up becoming in life is a "character" that has been cultivated and fashioned, one way or another; therefore, it is the cultivating and fashioning process that makes the man, all the required ingredients are already there.

As I write I am sure somewhere far away there is an institution disallowing a talented individual the chance to study art because he or she is starting too late. Or because of his status in society or her gender. Not long ago, it was thought that only men could be good artists. And they had to come from France and Italy! In my own experience, a very good friend of mine, about fifteen years ago, told me that I am pursuing art in America too late in my life. I was in my twenties. On three occasions, I have taken students who were told they didn't have what it takes to become artists. All of these three students went on to win the highest awards in the student juried shows at the National Academy School of Fine Arts. They gave me time, devotion and trust, and worked like crazy.

If by chance you are not too sure of your talent, I assure you that everyone at some point has been doubtful of his or her abilities. It is that doubt that makes us want to learn. Do not forget how many times Rodin failed, how crazy and untalented everyone thought Van Gogh was when he started. Yet now no one can doubt his passion and dedication. If by chance you think it is too late to pursue art, please don't believe it. All good teachers love inspired, devoted students who are willing to work; these teachers are aware of countless successful achievers who started late. In the arts, we hear so much of all those who started very young, but we don't hear of those who started young but got burned out later. If by chance you think you don't have what it takes, then go and offer to work with an accomplished instructor, tell him you are a Lemon and willing to have some fresh lemonade squeezed out of you. There is no human being who can't learn; if he has some desire and some passion for learning, anyone can improve himself. Of all the abilities a man needs to achieve success as an artist, talent is the most overrated. I often wonder, if talent is everything, then how come only those who work the hardest and think the most realistically become the greatest achievers. If you think you don't have enough talent, think again. All you need is the will to endure, the studio time to learn the skills, the willingness to search for knowledge and wisdom in books, plus good instructors and a logical, philosophical approach to the field. The only thing you cannot learn is what your subconscious mind has rejected. If the subconscious mind wants something, it sends forces that can help the mind and the body to achieve what it wants. The mind will provide the energy, the strength and the inspiration—all the necessary ingredients to make things happen.

How Much Passion Is Needed to Fulfill Your Dreams?

In mankind's progress, little has been accomplished without passion. Great achievements are possible when people have a passionate love for their field of expertise. Why else would a person who has the abilities and brains to make millions on Wall Street choose to become a nurse and end up with a lower income and less renown? Why else would a scientist choose to find ways to put thousands of songs on a small portable device while another chooses to study how cockroaches multiply in a basement? Why else would one young man choose to pursue law to help the underprivileged while another chooses to pursue music to entertain the populace? The simple reason is that we humans have a certain innate quest, driven by passion, to fulfill a certain destiny. We must feed this inner desire in order to feel worthy of living.

Figure 5

JOAQUIN BATISDA
y SOROLLA

*Hispanic Society
of America*

*For posters of Joaquin
Sorolla's work, call
(212) 926-2234 or visit:
www.hispanicsociety.org*

Passion is a reward given to us long before that destiny has been fulfilled. Passion is a reward like all other rewards—success, money, fame and recognition. But unlike the rewards one gets for something accomplished, passion is invisible and intangible. It is a reward granted us without any choice, in the form of a spell from the supreme intelligence. Passion is a reward embedded in our subconscious, secure within us until the duty is finished, and every little bit of the reward is fully enjoyed. We are no matches for the spell passion casts upon us. Monetary rewards may gratify us with the means to afford things; awards and recognition can please us with some fame and a certain sort of happiness in society, but passion alone gives us a more powerful emotion, and that imparts the supreme strength and enduring energy we need to fulfill our duty. The strength, love, and joy passion gives us have no limitations. Passion is what drives a person to sacrifice everything in order to achieve what that passion requires. With its great enthusiasm, passion is like a bribe from the gods, enticing us to do a particular work and to enjoy the work more than anyone else, without thought of either the sacrifices or rewards.

As we go about our daily business, there are several signals that lead us to claim this love and boundless enthusiasm in the service of our duty. All that is needed on our part is to lean toward that duty, to listen to our inner self and to look carefully for the clues. As part of the supreme intelligence's plan or design, everyone has some sort of passion assigned to him by means of which he will contribute to the well being of the universe. It is the universe's form of division of labor. For the universe to go on forever the seasons should not fail, and the books must be balanced at all costs. We must all contribute by fulfilling our particular duty. It is because of this that we cannot accept the theory that some are created with more talent and passion than others. Not finding your passion and fulfilling your duty does not mean the creator has overlooked your responsibilities, and therefore you can just breath free air. It is in the interest of the creator, the architect of the universe, that the universe go on forever, and, for that matter, that no one should be left behind. It is also in the creator's interest that we should have inner love and strength, everlasting joy and happiness while we work. Without such an innate reward we will not fulfill our duty well. Ambition in a specific field without passion turns work into a nine-to-five job. Our passionate ambitions are, therefore, our special assigned duty.

The way to find your own passion is to ask yourself questions about what you like to do, and then narrow the possibilities down to just a few. Start by making a list of your own ideas. What did you dream of doing when you were a child or a teenager? Then ask your friends, your colleagues and your family what they think you like to do based on their observations of you. You might have ten lists by the time you're finished. After all the lists have been made, cancel out the ideas you definitely know you don't want to pursue.

You will know which of the ideas you don't like just because you are a human and it is not part of your genetic make up to like more than seven fields equally. There will be some things on the lists that will hold your interest more than others. And then there will be some things that you really won't want to cross out. These are the things that you will want to consider. Narrow this remaining list to three, five, or seven options. Hide the list for a week without looking at it, then consider what you can remember without too much effort. Follow your heart at the end of the day, really and honestly listen to yourself. There is always one thing that we'd like to pursue, but for some weird reason, we always find excuses why we shouldn't or can't pursue that field. We never, ever give that field a try. If you follow your heart you will not have to go too far to find your own passion.

If the reward is not claimed and the duty not fulfilled, the self-guilt and blame will be strong enough that no other rewards can be enjoyable. Generally, such unfulfilled people just seem bored and guilty; however, this form of boredom and guilt is a form of punishment from nature for not fulfilling your

Figure 6

JOAQUIN BATISDA y SOROLLA, *Portrait of Louis Comfort Tiffany*

Hispanic Society of America is a hidden treasure for artists interested in color and the impressionistic method. During my student days I was lucky enough to meet Markus Burke and Margaret O'Connors, their generosity and insight to the museums collections and Joaquin Sorolla helped me tremendously. It is a museum every artist should visit now and then.

For posters of Joaquin Sorolla's work, call (212) 926-2234 or visit: www.hispanicsociety.org

responsibility by contributing to life's division of labor. For those people, life will not be as enjoyable and rewarding as it is supposed to be. Some great achievements can be accomplished without passion, but it is more inspiring, adventurous, rewarding, and worthy of life's journey to achieve life's goals with passion.

Since passion is very elusive and intangible, you don't have to worry if you have it or not. The student, in particular, does not have to worry about having it or not. Sometimes the awareness of the passion comes to you slowly over time; therefore, the student should not wait for it before deciding on his vocation. There have been many great achievers whose passion developed once they were already in the field. But you can find what your passion is by using the above method.

There are other reasons why one does not necessarily need to have passion at the beginning of their education or training. Statistics show that over two-thirds of all successful people achieve success doing something they don't like. Less than one-third of successful people like what they do and one percent of this one-third is passionate about what they do. Whether this one percent entered their field with innate passion or discovered it after they were already in the field is hard to tell. Some people are very good and very successful at what they do but not passionate about it. But only passion will give you that overwhelming joy and love that nothing else—no reward, prize or recognition—can take the place of.

Before Enrolling in an Art Class
Self-Taught Students

Almost all students entering art school have done some painting and drawing on their own, working from their imagination, from life or by making copies. Some students working on their own prior to entering art school will have developed several useful skills that can be helpful, but sometimes they have also picked up habits that won't be helpful. In the beginning, almost any skill the student has learned on his own is better than no skill at all. But it is very important for the student to know that some sort of mental adjustment has to be made to studying professionally, and the student has to prepare himself by being aware that not all that he has learned will be helpful or useful. This will make the transition easier from the free, self-taught environment to the more structured study that schools offer. In most professional and traditional studios, the student will have to unlearn some things in order to make room for new things.

For example, copying a photograph or a painting at a museum or copying a painting from a reproduction is totally different from painting from a live model, but it is hard to know this if the student hasn't worked from life. Also, copying drawings from other drawings is very different from drawing from life. Even copying in order to reproduce an image is not the same as copying in order to learn from the image. Photos and museum works, being flat, are much easier to work from than the live model, where the illusion of three-dimensional nature has to be created on a two-dimensional surface. Most experienced teachers will advise the student not to worry, just to put aside what they have learned prior to entering the studio and start afresh with an open mind. If the student is receptive and open-minded, he will learn more quickly than if he tries to hang on to past experiences.

Copies made by a student might make it look as if he has more experience than the average beginning student working from life in a studio. This experience will often make the student take a couple of steps backward before going forward. The caution here is for the student to constantly remind himself that the copies will always look better than most works done from life by new students, Because with copies, all the difficult technical problems have been solved already by the original artist, so there is no comparison with the works by students who are still learning what to do. Copies will always look more impressive than student works; this is another reason why the student should not worry too much about the samples he shows in the beginning. It would be better if he were to appreciate that he now has the privilege of having the opportunity to start off learning from a professional, the proper beginning. I had the hardest time adjusting after I moved to the United States from Europe. There, I had been a professional getting paid for my skills and experience at a very young age. I had had lots of freedom to do as I wished. I had been included in group exhibitions with some of the best painters in Italy. Then, when I came to the U.S., I realized that it is not what I have done, but rather how much I know. This realization made me see myself as a student once again.

There are several good ethical qualities that the self-taught artist develops, yet there are also some habits the self-taught pick up along the way that are not compatible with the structured learning environment that is best for learning to be a good artist. This structured environment is always advantageous for the self-taught artist who will consciously accept the reality that his new beginning can make him into a better artist.

Talent and Other Requirements

Studying art seriously is not that different from studying for any other profession, such as architecture, medicine, business or law; the only difference is in the nature of the subject studied. In other professions, the student will have to have an objective idea of what is involved so he can plan ahead. For exam-

Figure 7 MUSETTE MORGAN, *Flowers, oil on panel*

ple, most students pursuing professional courses will have to figure out how to pay for four to six years of tuition. And they will also need the stamina to endure for that length of time. How will they afford housing and books? The rest of their expenses are standard and apply to any field. There are similar expenses to consider at any college, and it usually takes four years to graduate.

For the student of traditional art, studying at an art academy or privately, there is no one-size-fits-all scenario: such a student could spend from two to ten years studying. There usually is no college housing for traditional art students. They cannot budget precisely for materials and books because they cannot tell beforehand exactly what they will need. Each of the professional artists who are teaching the student will have his own requirements. There might be extra fees for props, models and studio rentals—fees that can't be anticipated. At college the art student can plan ahead with fixed numbers; the traditional approach to learning art is unlike that of the college educational system. This affects both practical matters and what is learned. Simply because the curriculum is not the same, college students often don't get the same experience as those art students studying in a traditional environment. This is why serious college graduates who want to be practicing traditional artists may end up continuing to study privately in a more traditional set-up after graduation, adding about three years of traditional teaching to their four years of college for a total of seven years.

It is because of this that the student who wants to learn how to paint traditionally needs to plan and prepare to use his talent and mind effectively, to try and save as many years as possible, which will mean saving on tuition as well. Also, he needs to plan to be ready to approach galleries as soon as he advances into the professional arena.

It takes a set number of credits and a certain grade point average to get a degree at most colleges. By paying the tuition, working hard and following the curriculum, the average student can get his degree in four years. In the traditional arts, the average student can save some years by practicing more or by taking on projects like copying paintings, or just by drawing and painting at home. Indirectly sacrificing some early freedom and fun, he can learn to find joy in learning.

Studying to Pursue Artistic Vocation

"Great works and great people meet nothing strong enough to oppose their destiny." —Cecilia Beaux

Students should be logical in their study plans.
What is the difference between an art student, an artist and a professional artist?
Learning will be so easy if the student can clearly define these differences.

I was recently in India, where I saw a group of men carving an intricate sculpture of beautiful wooden elephants. As I watched them sculpt and create, I learned that the design for the sculpture had been handed down through a family of artists for generations. I became curious about the Indian, or Eastern, perspective on artists compared to the American, or Western, perspective. I made a comment to one of the craftsman about the exceptional quality of the piece. I said, "You are such good artists to make something so beautiful." To which one of the men replied, "Oh no, we are not yet artists. The master who created the original is the artist, we are still learning. We could not be considered artists until we learn some important basic skills!" I thought to myself that here in America just being able to use the materials alone is enough for a student to call himself an artist. But like other trades, the student needs to learn and understand some basics and go through the learning stages before he can become a sincere and honest artist.

Traditionally, art was considered a trade. As in all other trades, such as that of mason, carpenter and electrician, it is this understanding of learning that humbles and encourages the serious art student. There are stages of professional development. One begins the study of the craft as an apprentice. The apprentice mostly observes the work of a master. The student is given projects designed for learning. After a number of years, the apprentice "graduates" to the level of journeyman. The journeyman engages in the trade, or craft, but only under the supervision of a master. It is not for many years that the journeyman can himself be considered a master. Nowadays in the west, art as a craft or trade has fallen out of fashion. It has become demeaning to art in America to consider it a trade. Because the public condones this practice, the art student suffers from not being able to use his potential talent to its fullest. He is not challenged and he has no standard to look up to.

Thinking about what art is, about what the layman thinks art is, and what we know about art, it might seem that no plan is needed for studying art, that the field is too abstract and personal, and therefore no education is needed before becoming an artist. But knowing how all great artists went about acquiring education, experience and knowledge about the field, one realizes how important it is to have an education. Thinking about what the world has become, how expensive the cost of living is and how valuable time, the art student is left with the conclusion that the gains he will get from planning his education are much too important to take for granted, and the efficiency of a creative mind in times like these can only ease some hardships.

People with goals succeed because they know where they are going. It is as simple as that. —Earl Nightingale

For the student, the truth of this adage is a reminder that success follows from plans that target specific goals, and all plans come from ideas, or from dreams, about achieving specific ambitions. The idea of becoming an artist should be followed up by a plan aimed at achieving that goal. Before enrolling in an art program, the student should figure out a plan of who to study with or what kind of education he needs, where he might find a mentor or go for professional advice, and how many years he will need to invest in his studies to get the right education.

In some ways, because of the uniqueness and abstract quality of Fine Art, there are no clear-cut answers to these questions, and it would be very wrong to suggest that there are easy answers. The whole point for the student of putting these questions into consideration is to stick to his dreams and make a plan that will form a part of his strategic approach to the future. That plan will help the student prepare and make him aware of what he is doing, thus preventing him from following the normal course of jumping in to pursue art while hoping that all will be well. Sometimes, a handful of lucky students get some useful guidance, but more often the average student has to learn the hard way. A dream of becoming a good artist is very good; it keeps the fire burning, while a plan with specifications makes the dream attainable.

My first humbling professional exposure in New York City came to me by way of a statistic I had read. That statistic was the reason that I put all that I knew aside, and started to pursue research into what it takes to survive in a city like New York. The statistic was in an account of starving artists in New York—to me it asked if I have what it takes to pursue art in the Big Apple. According to this statistic, there are more than 240,000 artists in New York City, but only 3% of that number actually make a living through their art. And only 1% of those successful artists can actually be considered "good" artists. Most people think that the majority of artists don't succeed or make a living at their art because they do not have enough talent, or because they are not well trained. The reality is that most artists are uninformed about how to prepare for their field of study. In fact, it is not a question of talent, or luck, or even moti-

Figure 8 SAM ADOQUEI, *Oranges and Azaleas, oil on canvas*

vation. It is a matter of how to pursue a living in a serious and a tough field—a field that requires serious guidance. These artists are not doing the right home-work, or asking the right questions, such as:

How should an art student approach learning?

Do successful masters have some secret learning habits that art students can adopt?

How does an artist master the rules of the Five Worlds of Art so that he can have some control over his artistic destiny?

How can the artist differentiate between the romantic and idealistic life of the artist and his practical life?

I will keep hammering home the idea that the purpose of a school is to provide all that that the student did not learn prior to enrollment. It is natural and logical that all art students hope to learn well in order to create works that will be worthy of exhibition Then, with successful exhibitions, the artist can gain enough recognition and a large-enough following that his future will be secured. These are the dreams of students in all fields. What went wrong for the art student and how did he miss the bus? Did he rely too much on school or spend too much time dreaming and hoping, wishful thinking instead of thinking right, or searching for the right approach to learning? Did he relax too much because there was no one to check on his performance? Has he become a real victim of modern society's freedom, the freedom that says all artists are entitled to do as they wish. Yes, artists are entitled to do as they wish, but only those artists who are educated and experienced professionals can handle such freedom.

Perhaps the art student has never asked himself such important questions as: What are my reasons for studying art? Why should I study art and how should I study it?

How does a serious student plan his studies?

Is there a strategy I can use?

Should I seek to find out by research and advice?

The new student will need knowledge of the journey he must take to become an artist—the craft and the techniques of Drawing, Values, Form, Color, Composition, Design and Cultured Taste. These make up the core foundation of technical efficiency. Even though the student might not master these areas in a year or two, it helps to know how important they are and to at least quickly focus on them. The student should at least learn the basics of all the genres: Portrait, Landscape, Figure and Still Life. As a student, make it a point to learn the art and science of Portraiture as well as the art and science of Still life, the art and science of all kinds of drawing, and the art and science of all the areas above. The art and science of solving problems—that's why we go to school.

Portraiture, Figure Painting, Still Life and Landscape

Portraiture: Solving a portrait problem is interesting, analytical, mathematical and scientific. Painting a portrait is not just painting a face; if the artist is sensitive enough he can see everything on an individual face, from the four seasons, history and religion to all of life's experiences. Sensitivity is a part of the student's abilities that needs cultivating. Making a portrait is not just copying

the facial features. Figure Painting: Figurative art develops the careful analytical, mathematical and scientific senses; it is like the portrait. Still Life: Studying still life develops the technical senses, the handling of technique and almost all the other areas of technical problems, such as texture, space, atmosphere, mood and light. Landscape: Learning landscape develops the sense of freedom—of taking chances and not worrying too much about details.

During the student period, avoid styles, tricks and gimmicks. Know what to require from yourself.

The student should also know that being in class every day and drawing and painting every day doesn't necessarily make him a great artist. Being an artist requires the student to be aware of certain goals, to know what he is

Figure 9

JOHN SINGER SARGENT, *An Artist in His Studio 1904, American (1856-1925), oil on canvas,*

56.2x72.07cm (22 ⅛ x 28 ⅜ in.) Museum of Fine Arts, Boston

working for; the student should make sure his drawing and painting are exercises leading toward an understanding of technical solutions that will equip him with an understanding of how to solve problems. Time is often wasted because a student works on irrelevant projects. Students get confused between painting and producing canvases, between painting as a project, or as a process leading to the understanding of a technical method or a particular aspect of technique.

The student must train himself not to get too attached to the particular works he does during the time he is working on technical exercises nor to take criticism too personally. Always the student should remember that he is a student, and not yet a painter or a mature artist. He should always understand what kind of artwork he is producing—whether it is a creative work, a commercial work, or if it is an innovative work or an experimental work. Each of these areas should train a particular part of his talent or senses. The student should learn to know the differences among these areas in order to be more practical about learning. Doing creative artwork develops your abilities to create work that suits your personal desires. You don't have to follow reality too much. Commercial artwork involves the artist and a second party. Both have to be happy, although most often the second party is the one who has to be happier because he is the one who will be paying. Experimental or innovative artwork tries out new ideas in the hopes of discovering new ways of creating—this type of work is not always suitable for beginners.
Develop the important and appropriate skills: creative skills, artistic skills, commercial skills and technical skills as well as good taste. Students should also develop discipline and ethical qualities.

The art student should avoid thinking of specializing in a particular area while he is a student; rather he should acquire general skills in broad areas, and only specialize when he has acquired confidence and can understand the rules involved in solving artistic problems (he must master the craft, so he will be able to recognize and fix technical mistakes). His development as an artist depends on this mental power, or ability; he should develop his sensitivities in order to be able to see or find beauty in nature and be able to make a creative work out of anything. Art students sometimes allow their emotions to get in the way of what is right for them; they need to learn that studying is now their main priority—to help them develop the right attitude towards their work so that they can produce art under whatever their personal circumstances happen to be.

Be Reasonable and Realistic:
Your Talent and the Real World

Aspiring artists must understand the world that exists around them. It is good to have artistic passion but it is wiser to be realistic and to remember that today is as important as tomorrow, and that tomorrow depends on today. Until we solve today's problems and prepare for the future, tomorrow will be vague. We may wake up one day and realize that tomorrow has arrived, and we haven't learned that which we need to live a creative life.

Most students are naïve when it comes to pursuing art as a vocation. Only a handful have sat down with a professional artist and asked for objective advice and guidance regarding such questions as:

What should I do to become an artist, from the start of my studies to becoming a professional? How should I go about acquiring the knowledge and skills that are needed?

What should I, the student, expect from studying? How can I monitor my progress?

I have been painting and working from such-and-such time, and these are the works I have produced and have to show—how many years should it realistically take me to be able to acquire enough additional skill in order to

build my future career from this base toward a specialty? (If the student follows a particular course with a specific curriculum, then, depending on the specialty, it should take three to seven years after learning the basics. But if there is no specific curriculum, it will take more years. This is why it pays to prepare and to be informed.)

Just to have these questions at the back of your head is enough to start you off as a student. Trying to find your own answers is even better. Almost all professional artists will have different experiences but by speaking to a couple of them, the student will have a more realistic idea of what path will best suit his personal journey.

There are three types of students who will eventually become artists after some years of study. The traits these students possess are almost identical. A high percentage of them will walk into art school with their own innocent plan without any input from a professional. This group of students often has the hardest time learning unless by sheer chance some caring professional advises and guides them along the way.

Then there are a few students who will walk into a school or a studio willing to do everything right: listen to what is being taught, complete every assignment, spend time acquiring more knowledge from books and magazines, and by asking advice from the professional. With such a work ethic, these students will study with an idea in mind of what should be done, even though that idea is not an exact understanding of the science of learning art that all professionals artists use in approaching art. This group of students will become good because they already possess the innate habit of learning by working hard. Because of this inherent habit that this group possesses, they are more likely to be realistic and to follow the steps that successful artists have taken in history. The only problem is that what worked 100 years ago, 50 years ago or even 25

Figure 10

HENRY FANTIN LATOUR
French, 1836-1904,
Flowers on a Table,
1865

Museum of Fine Arts,
Boston. Bequest of
John T. Spaulding
48.540

years ago, will not work today. Therefore this group's chance of surviving as artists is diminished. They will acquire some skills because they have followed the prescribed program, but without clear specific goals based on modern reality, their fate will depend on luck. For example, what if the program they followed isn't good enough? What if the skills they developed are too personal or too unrealistic? What if they are learning unnecessary skills? What if they are specializing in a style that looks too similar to someone else's?

Then there is the last group, which represents only a handful of the students studying art. These have the traits of both group "A" and group "B." They know what abilities they have; they know that they can be good, and they are willing to work very hard and sacrifice some time. They are realistic in that they know they can only be rewarded according to how much they invest in the art. They are also realistic enough to realize that the art and science of any field can only be known by professionals who are practicing in the field, who have followed the path and who now have experience. This group invests their talent and time, and trusts to fate and luck in the hope that natural law will reward them according to that investment. Work hard, think right, plan well and work the plan. This handful of students will either consult a professional or will find such a person for a mentor before starting to study, or they will find guidance once they start and eventually learn to be realistic themselves. All their years of studying art will be devoted to gradual mastery, from basics to complex techniques—from reading to research to museum visits to practicing the craft at their leisure. They will take their painting classes very seriously—to this group, the pursuit of art is as serious as any other profession. These students know that a painting studio where one can learn and acquire knowledge is more important than going to class to produce a painting. This group keeps checking on their progress with a professional or a mentor for the sake of focusing on what is important. This group always makes it to the professional level. They are always ready for luck to show up and with a little opportunity they excel. This is the group that follows art in the same way that other professionals—doctors, financial brokers, architects—pursue their fields. This group knows what it takes to be creative, productive, inventive and commercial. They often have the humility to consult other professionals with questions regarding growth when they start practicing.

Suggestions for These Groups

If you find yourself falling into the first category, take a moment to consider the time and tuition you are planning to invest in the study of art. Consult one or more professional artists regarding what you have in mind. Be honest and they will be more than happy to share some invaluable advice with you even though it may not be as you had imagined. Give that advice some reasonable consideration and by the time you have spoken to several artists, you will have an idea of how you should approach your learning. Don't be discouraged if in the beginning the advice sounds too rigid, sometimes it might even sound like your freedom is being taken away. Just think about the end result. Think about the financial investment, too; acknowledge the reality of your loss if you set about learning without a clear plan. Remember at the end it will be more your loss than anyone else's. Also remember that three, or even five, years of devoting yourself to acquiring skill in doing something you like so much is not that great a sacrifice.

The idea of different worlds that each member of society lives in is not a myth to professional people. Any professional person has his or her professional world, which consists of his or her professional friends, and then his or her family life, the two of which often cannot be mixed together. If you are among those who see art as a beautiful game in which the winner gets his wishes, hopes and dreams granted, know that it takes three to seven years of mastering the rules of the game in order for you to play the game happily, and to be rewarded fairly. Aim to be part of group "B" in hopes to be able to move to the 1% group.

Your Contribution to Society

In the long run the student should aim to be able to be of some use to society. He can ask himself, "What kind of services should I perform or provide for society, for art enthusiasts and laymen, so that in return I will be rewarded with the means to afford life's necessities? So I can live and create and fantasize as I wish?"

Since the world around us is so different from the world of the artists we read about we artists of today cannot afford to live and act like those artists who lived in the past. Society has changed for the betterment of mankind. What we have today is the best the world has to offer.

The romantic ideas the student might have, that make him think that studying art does not require serious planning, and, therefore, that there is no need to worry about these questions, are the same uninformed, romantic ideas and twisted views that will lead that artist to make unrealistic decisions in his approach to studying art.

Summarized

- Almost all artists start to study art with some kind of idealistic view, with ideas that are far from reality, ideas often programmed by romantic stories written by clever writers.
- The artist should not let his artistic passion and fantasies allow him to overlook the realities of the practical and physical world run by man. Planning is very good; it prepares the student for what is to come and helps him know what is important during the student period.
- Find pleasure in learning and seeking knowledge—be knowledgeable about the art of studying art.
- Find an established studio where you can learn and acquire professional experience. Remember your duties as a student and what is required of you. There are no grades and therefore there is no one to monitor your progress or deceive you, no one but yourself.
- There is no fulfilling joy greater than total control and command over the craft of painting and the knowledge and wisdom of the field that mastery will give you.
- Always remember the noble cause of an artist.

As the saying goes, "Choose the work you love and you will never work a day in your life." One might think that because of this mantra artists are happy or at least not as frustrated as people in other fields. After all, we all chose to make art because we love doing it, yet, funny enough, the agony art brings is often very challenging and sometimes very difficult. Sometimes you wonder why the artist chose to be in the artistic field. The pain is even worse when the artist realizes that pain was never a part of the package he bargained for. Art being a way of life will always bring some challenges. If the artist dares to dream big, the challenges will be even more difficult.

Unluckily, in modern times the challenges do not occur because the artist is chasing unattainable dreams, or wants to live in an artistic fantasy world. Most of the difficulties and agonies come to the artist because he went into the field without adequate preparation. He never bothered to find out the nature of the field, but rather jumped into it, hoping any realistic and practical problems would solve themselves.

To start an artistic journey is a serious life decision. Without a realistic understanding and careful planning and research into the field, starting such a journey stacks the odds against the student.

No matter how much any artist dreams or fantasizes about what art is, at the end of the day the artist will always live in this practical and physical world created by man, a world that exists because of all the elements that make it function: farmers, physicians, landlords, all looking for fees as rewards for their services. For the artist to live he also will have to be rewarded for providing some sort of direct or indirect service, so society can gain from his efforts. And the plan needed to assist an artist to live in this physical world requires figuring out what it takes to have the skills needed to provide a certain kind of service worth rewarding—a service that will be useful enough that there are people willing to reward the artist by exchanging part of their income for his artwork. Or at least exchanging the things the artist needs for his artworks. This is why the artist can dream all he wants, but he should have a solid, practical approach to dealing with the world in order to be able to afford to dream, create and envision the future. The romantic stories that often inspire the artist are just romantic lies, stories that are only good for reading and to sell books and make a profit for those who do not live the artist's life.

The romantic lives, ideas and stories we read about great artists, even if they happened, did not happen because those great artists didn't know better or planned it so. The great artists didn't live their lives so that books could be written about them. Their lives happened naturally, spontaneously, without following a scripted story.

In most learning environments, the student might have to put aside who he is in order to be a good student. He might have to adjust his attitude so that while still a student he can think and work like a student. As simple as this might seem, this adjustment of attitude has caused many students a lifetime of frustration.

Figure 11

SIGMUND ABELES,
Horsing Around

CHAPTER ◂O2◂

UNDERSTANDING HOW ARTISTS THINK

Artist's Evolution, from Natural Talent to Professional Artist

Beginning art students will need to be introduced to Drawing, Portrait Painting, Still Life, Basic Artistic Anatomy and Composition. New students will also learn the basic ways of approaching painting, including such painting methods as grisaille and the block-in method. Then, beginning art students must get into the practice of doing research on art. They should visit museums, participate in summer workshops in landscape painting, and make it a practice to read as many books about art as they can.

Finally, the beginning art student must understand the value of finding a professional mentor to advise them as they go through their studies. And, finally, an art student must begin to discipline himself to draw on his own. In this way he will come to understand how and when to practice. A beginning art student must start to use his free time to become better at what he does, which is accomplished mainly by drawing, learning the basic proportions, and by painting still lifes and copying the paintings of the masters.

The Advanced Art Student

First, the advanced art student should spend his time studying general art history. He should develop an interest in understanding theoretical principles, as well as the reasons for the different movements and legacies of the past. His studies should help him to not only learn about the field, but also help him to understand the theoretical ideas that make good painting. For example, the Impressionists loved nature and believed that the natural world was more beautiful than what could be imagined. This idea helped them to see beauty in everyday life. The abstract artist believes in not spelling out everything for the viewer. Knowledge, combined with hands-on work in the studio under a professional artist, is what separates advanced students from ordinary students or self-taught artists.

Second, the advanced art student must acquire knowledge about contemporary art. He should know what goes on around him. He should develop a professional work ethic; the quest to improve himself should fill his thoughts daily—this is his main goal.

Third, the advanced art student needs to develop humility and respect toward his mentor and other good painters he happens to meet. Thus, other artists will feel comfortable sharing their ideas with him. He should learn to ask good questions when he meets artists who are more advanced in their work than he is. As the student improves, advice from other artists will be very important to him, and will be needed more than ever. Because these artists are already in the professional world that the student hopes to enter, they only impart such knowledge to those who deserve it.

The Transition Between Student and Professional—The Serious Artist

First, during his transition to a professional, the serious student will continue to study historical works of art seriously. Second, he will also study works in galleries by his contemporaries, and he should not form negative criticisms of the works, but rather develop the habit of finding good qualities in the work of contemporaries while at the same time being able to differentiate good work from bad. The serious artist will learn more from searching for the good qualities in other artists' works (even their bad works); this will be more beneficial to him than bashing those works. Finally, the serious artist will put together a portfolio suitable for presentation to those galleries he desires to be represented by.

Figure 12 ANN MARIE BUENAVENTURA, *Drawing of a Old Man, graphite*

THE FIVE WORLDS OF CREATIVE ARTISTS

In order to understand and accept the reasons why you, the student, should acquire skills and be practical about studying art, be aware that artists live in five different worlds.

These five worlds illustrate how most artists think about the field before entering it seriously.

Our Inner Artistic World (the inner world is personal).

The Real World (the practical world).

The Outside World (our artistic circle, plus the realistic and commercial world)

The Future World (our dreams and aspirations and mortality). Tomorrow will come but we have no idea what it may bring. Whether we will use the skills of yesterday and today to survive in tomorrow's world or we will have to adjust, or adopt, we have no idea.

The Fantasy World (dreamland). We dream of greatness and a successful life.

1. The Artistic World Within Us.

Our inner world is very passionate, idealistic and sometimes romantic. It often disagrees with reality and thereby interferes with the growth of our realistic mind. Because the romantic and idealistic mind is not practical or logical, it tends to be more unwilling to be challenged, to adopt new ideas or to change. All these things prevent talent from growing. Because we only think selfishly, we find our thoughts and ideas incompatible with the world around us. An art student should be aware of these traits, that they come naturally to all artists, and then work hard in developing and controlling his mind so that he can accept wholeheartedly that some freedom will need to be sacrificed in order to acquire the skills and way of thinking it takes to become a competent artist. When he can make such a deal with his idealistic subconscious mind, then the art student will find it necessary to accept the road that leads to acquiring information, knowledge, experience and wisdom for the fulfillment of his artistic vocation.

2. The Real World

How realistically do you see the world around you? At first by nature, through their idealistic and romantic minds, art students dream a lot about their higher hopes and wishes. It is a good thing that art students have great hopes and wishes, and that every artist has bigger dreams than anyone else. No technique, experience or knowledge is needed to solve the problems of these big artworks. The best imaginable strength that can keep a dream alive is the power of passion, hopes and dreams, that is the fire that keeps us going. Without these traits, we might as well give up. It's these dreams and hopes that inspire us to keep going. But it is much, much easier to accomplish any dream if the artist has some sense of the practical and uses common sense in the beginning. Accidents and luck have some role to play in the things scientists accomplish, but not so much as the science of achieving goals.

If you find yourself illogical about the real and practical world, remember that, after all, you are a human being and you can't live without the important human needs: food, shelter, clothing, medicine, etc. Also remember that the world around us has its own laws that make it live on. To be part of that world, one should learn to understand its laws, the laws of nature, religion, science, people and business, etc. Don't wish or dream too much for the future. Without being unrealistic about the existence of things around us, combine all your healthy wishes, dreams and hopes into investing in your talent and in the acquisition of knowledge, experience and wisdom. If your art contributes to society, or to the art enthusiasts around you, then you are rewarded honestly, and more so if you honestly make yourself useful to the world around you.

3. The Outside World

It is not easy for the artist to realize how many worlds he lives in. Even if he does understand that we live in these five worlds, he often doesn't make the effort to understand all those worlds, so that he can be an artist and still live compatibly with his surroundings, still create art and continue becoming a better artist. Without realizing it, we innocently tend to choose the ideal romantic lifestyle that is actually only a creation of writers and publishers to sell books. Take a look at movies about artists or musicians, and you will see that the pain is romanticized so much that it leads the student to want to live the life of the artist in the movie. But ask the artist who was in the movie or the story if they enjoyed their life then. They will say it was no joke. If Van Gogh's romantic life is wonderful for us to read about or to talk about, remember who thinks the story is great and wonderful and romantic. Not Van Gogh but the public, plus the writers and publishers and those making profits from his painful and tragic life.

Figure 13 SAMUEL ADOQUEI, *Social Studies.*

The average artist with romantic ideas may want to live the life of Vincent Van Gogh—until one day he realizes that he does not have a brother to support him, and he didn't die at thirty-seven years old. He is now forty-five years of age, heading towards sixty, and living in an expensive competitive city, not a village in the south of France. And he has to take care of several important natural needs. The fact that we are unique entities means we will each have our own baggage to deal with.

The Outside World is the realistic world, whether we like it or not. It is the world that we will grow in both physically (as all humans do) and artistically (as all artists wish). It is this world that provides us with shelter, food, and health—all at a price. Whatever the landlord charges those living in his building, we have to pay, just as the restaurant asks what it wants for a meal. The Outside World makes its rules and we have no choice but to follow them. This gives us some idea of what will be expected from artists, and it even tells us how many rooms are for lucky artists, and how many rooms will be available for hard-working artists, and how many rooms for well-equipped artists. The Outside World will often treat preferably those artists willing to take chances and contribute to it. After all, the Outside World has been telling us since birth all we need to do if we want to live within it. Best of all, it also tells us how to find the information we need and the secrets of living. We can go looking for the information and secrets and use them if we want to live well. And for these Laws of Living within the Outside World, all professionals in every field have no choice but to search for the secrets and information necessary. With knowledge and experience, in order to live harmoniously with the Outside World, and in order to create as one wishes, we all have to be aware of these realistic facts and accept them whole-heartedly, and enjoy the process of learning in order to use them for what we want. Not being aware of them or not accepting them is the beginning of the war between the artist and the Outside World.

4. The Future World

If you are a member of the group who see art as a beautiful game where the winner gets his wishes, hopes and dreams granted, then aim to become artists who are practical and logical about life. Prepare for school, be realistic and see school as a place to acquire skill, experience and knowledge. Find a well-grounded professional artist or a mentor. Develop your enthusiasm for learning. Enjoy learning while still securing your dream profession. Don't worry about the future, even though history judges harshly, it is still kind to honest, hard-working artists.

5. The Fantasy World

Our artistic fantasy world is made up of all the big dreams we have, from getting the best artistic education to creating amazing, timeless artworks. We dream of showing in the best galleries or museums and of being famous as well as of immortality where we sit side by side with Michelangelo and Leonardo da Vinci and other great artists that we admire. We imagine having sensible conversations with our heros. These dreams are fantasies and will remain so. Being able to dream is the greatest of gifts, however. Imagine our lives without dreams.

Learning to Paint from Books

It is inevitable that new students will start learning from art books, as art books are more accessible and convenient than art classes. The most important reason for this is that new students are experimenting, trying out various methods, or are just curious.

I have seen several good self-taught artists who learned everything they know from following technical books. There are several situations when the student has no any other choice but to use books, such as lack of time, remote location, convenience and lack of money.

There are hundreds of great books on technique, and it would take several pages to mention them all and recommend some, but this chapter is not at all about books or materials to use, but rather it is about considering the use of art books. It is not a bad idea if the student's means of studying are limited. There is nothing at all wrong with using books.

The only caution about using books is that the student should be extremely careful with the kind of book he chooses. Most professional instructors will not agree that all books are good. That is because some of these books contradict the teaching of the instructor. For example, if Monet wrote a book on landscape painting, it would be very difficult for that book to be read or used by a student of Jean-Auguste-Dominique Ingres. But by the same token students of Van Gogh, Pissaro and Cézanne might gain some pointers from Monet's book. All teachers should always have some books they highly recommend, and when in doubt the student should always check with the teacher.

It is also not helpful for a student to think he can gain more information by combining contradictory techniques and ideas learned from books—this is the reason why so many students do not acquire solid, reliable skills. When learning from books, it is also very important to focus on a very few selected books that are in the same category. For example, when learning portraiture don't try to get every book on the subject. Choose two or three at most that teach the same technique. If you like the technique of Sargent, then get a book or two that discusses the alla prima technique, and if you like Rembrandt, get books that teach the techniques of Rembrandt. The same advice applies to landscape painting. When the student becomes a mature artist with total control over his materials, then he can buy as many books as he wants for reference sources.

Figure 14

SAMUEL
ADOQUEI,
*Sand Point at
Twilight*

Reality of the World

Just the fact that you are reading this book and have gotten this far is a sign
that you are curious about wanting to grow, and that means you want to find
out what you can do to learn well, and to improve yourself. You would like to
do as well as you can as an artist and as a student—to get the best out of your
student period. This means that you are following the path of all great artists of
the past and present, acquiring knowledge, gathering wisdom and creating in
order to enhance humanity. A pattern that is followed with such a realistic and
logical approach cannot go wrong. But before all these dreams, first and fore-
most, the artist has to take care of paying his landlord, buying his groceries and
clothing, and every now and then, getting together the money for a visit to his
doctor to take care of that human machine that assists him in pursuing those big
dreams.

Nature does not reward an individual artist just because he dreams; many
artists have dreamt their big dreams long before you did. Life will reward you
because you have made convincing arguments that you deserve a particular

reward—more than the other artists who want that same reward.

If you are in the group of students that thinks that just by doing the right thing you will achieve your goals, that working hard is good enough—well, it's true, you might achieve your goals, but too many things in your life will rely too much on luck. Here are a couple of things you can keep in consideration. Acquire enough information so that you can differentiate between style and technique, or skill. Style is the unique personal way an individual artist's work looks. Everyone has a style but not everyone has skill, or technique.

Technique is a method used to solve a problem; technique might include the methods by which an illusion is created, using certain effects, or an illusion of three dimensions, or just a soft mood. Technique in some ways seems the same as style but it is very different. For example, technically Van Gogh and Gauguin might use the same methods to solve problems but nevertheless they create a different look on their canvases. Skill refers to the level of mastery with which an artist handles complex technical problems.

Know and understand the Outside World, don't ignore or avoid it. Don't think that modern civilization is bad, try to understand modern civilization and make it work in your favor.

Ask for advice from someone who is successful in the field. Every good artist has once worked like, or even copied, another artist. Don't let public opinion force you to do the wrong thing by thinking otherwise. If you do, you will be sacrificing your uniqueness.

Almost any professional goes through similar stages before reaching maturity, from learning to understand the field (the student stage), then experimenting to find which branch of the field best suits his temperament (experimental stage), to making a profession out of the branch he likes: portraiture, still life, landscape, etc. The professional, or mature, stage is reached when you either do exactly what you want instead of searching for yourself, or just do whatever pays the bills. After school there are so many more things to do that a student never has to regret the time he gave up to go to school.

This book is only about what is necessary for the art student. It is not that important to go into detail here about things that will come after art school but it pays for the student to know that school is just a little part of the artist's life. So while you are a student, make the best of getting what is important from your education—do the best you can before moving on to pursue the artistic dream. The first stage is about education and acquiring education. The deci-

Figure 15

LUCAS CRANACH,
(German, 1472-1553)

Figure 16

SAMUEL ADOQUEI,
*Legacy of Dr. Martin
Luther King, tritych*

sions you will make and how you go about achieving the necessary education
and skills are what this book is about.

You have to be aware that your goal as an art student, who is not yet an
artist, is to believe that you are working toward becoming an artist. Foster your
enthusiasm. Enjoy the adventures of learning and the fun of growing. Bear in
mind the enthusiasm of just knowing that you are among the 1%; that in itself
is everything. It brings with it the freedom to do as you wish, while allowing
you to focus on your goals, and the rewards are fair.

The student has to be aware that he or she will have to sacrifice two, four,
five, even up to seven years, in order to gain the freedom that professionals
have. If the student is given his or her artistic freedom while still in school, he
or she will spend the rest of his/her artistic years frustrated.

CHAPTER ⊀O3⊀

THE ADVANTAGES OF YOUR PAST PROFESSION

The Advantages and Disadvantages to Students of Having Other Professional Backgrounds

We are all conditioned by our surroundings, our education, our profession, our gender and our age. I call this our frame of reference. Our beliefs, preferences, judgments and discriminations are processed through the filter of our surroundings, gender, experiences, education and age. We carry this filter wherever we go, and it affects the decisions we make and helps us make them. The filter is fluid and impressionable—it changes with us as we grow. It changes even as we become aware of it, and start to control it. Gaining control over our filtered knowledge is how we move on to a new enhanced, upgraded filter. This self-knowledge helps us bring extra experience to our new education.

In order to grow, it is necessary that we change and adapt our filter. We have to be aware of the filter that we carry, and we must remind ourselves that we have already filtered through our frame of reference our current knowledge of art and the study of art before we even enter art school. This filtering should not interfere with our real studying experience. What we know or think—or what has been previously processed through our filter—should not be fixed and static, so unmoving that we do not have space for all the new experiences we encounter. We should always take the opportunity to learn from our new experiences. We should always take the opportunity to clean or change our filter. What we like or dislike, what is popular, what is classy or what we consider worthy or important, impacts our study of art. The purpose of our education is

to fill our toolbox with as many problem-solving tools as possible—to broaden our frame of reference, to add on, change, or to create an entirely new filter. Students from different backgrounds receive and respond to art classes differently.

We become what we have been practicing for years, chances are that after three to five years we will start to live and behave the lifestyle we have now been aiming at and practicing and that after seven to ten years we will fully live the life of our chosen profession.

Figure 17

The author at fourteen painting billboards in Nigeria. The smallest panel I ever worked on during these years was over 8-feet in width and height. Before this job I used to design and hand silk screen T'shirts and jerseys for soccer teams. It is at this period that I learned working with clients.

The way we do things, solve problems and see life or respond to life depends on what we have been doing for 7 to 10 years. A doctor, an architect, a dancer, a scientist or a businessman will respond to different things when driving through the city or the countryside. He will respond differently to the various images in the changing landscape and for these same reasons students with a professional background who enter an art class will have different responses to lessons and painting subjects. A professional architect cannot be told to avoid seeing the structure of a tree or of a human being, and a doctor cannot be told to avoid thinking about the basic anatomy of a figure, because the average student with a certain background is unaware of how these things affect their learning. They will often go far before realizing the cause or reason why certain things cannot be done easily. If by chance, they are lucky enough to evaluate themselves, then chances are it will not take long for them to avoid letting their past slow their learning down.

Doctors with their scientific background tend to be very logical and often find it easy to learn the mechanics of the art and craft of painting. On the other hand, because of the difficulties of becoming a physician, they tend to under-rate the ethical process of becoming an artist. Often, they will quickly learn the technique and craft, but will not develop the sensitivity it takes to understand the essential qualities of nature or to develop respect for the subject. Because of this a student from a medical background will have to remind himself of the uniqueness of the art field and respect all aspects of it. Such a student should go through the learning stage without any preconceived notions in order to get everything he can from the field. If he does this, a student with a medical background has a fair chance to become as good as he or she wishes.

Architects tend to be very slow and meticulous in studying nature. They are very sensitive to the structure beneath things, and this helps them to pay attention to the organization of details. While this helps them with details, they often find it difficult to learn painting techniques that the painter needs to learn in order to suggest and unify information, or to take artistic liberties so that he can produce creative works rather than merely copying what he sees. During the early stage of the education of a student with an architectural background, he will find it helpful to study works by painters who are good at suggesting or unifying information, or by artists whose work shows creative freedom.

Students from business backgrounds tend not to take their time going through the learning process slowly in order to master the craft thoroughly. They tend to stop at the stage where they have understood enough to paint well but have not mastered it enough for the craft to become second nature to them. The mantra "Time is Money" often gets in their way. Too often for them it is for this reason that they tend to do well commercially but often lack the quality demanded to be a creative artist. Understanding the other side of art, the noble pursuit, the love of the field (or as great sportsmen put it "...the Love of the Game"), that passion to create in order to communicate, can help them get more from themselves than they bargained for.

Once, a student from a fashion background told me that it took her years of working in an artistic environment to start to find beauty in ordinary people and ordinary places. Until she adjusted her thinking on how to perceive the world as an artist does, she was unable to see beauty in the ordinary. Another student once asked me what there is in New York's Union Square to paint; she couldn't believe she had canceled a European painting workshop to work with me in one of the city's neighborhood parks. Later, after she had learned how to find beauty in nature, she started to enjoy painting both rural places and city parks.

Advantages of Your Professional Background

Every student who enters the field of art with a professional background, or any background that imparts skills, such as that of a plumber or a carpenter, has some advantages that can help him at school, probably more than he realizes. I cannot think of any background that can't help in the arts. The student might have to be aware of what he has, in order to make sure he takes into consideration how that background can help him. A carpenter will have fun stretching canvases, building his own easel, maybe making some money by stretching canvases for other students. I was amazed to see how seriously an army officer in painting class took assignments for homework; he regarded the assignments as if they were orders, finishing them on time and coming back for more.

An architect's sensibilities toward structure come in handy when learning how to construct a painting. Someone with a marketing background will have the advantage when it is time to market his work. A schoolteacher will inherently respond to learning. An architect, a physician, and a businessman, all have useful traits that can help in school; some students might forget to take advantage of their specialties, but to most students, utilizing them will come naturally.

In my teaching experience, students have benefited more from their backgrounds than not. Especially when I point it out to them. Their background helped speed up or simplify the learning process. For example, when a writer learns that composing a picture is like plotting a story, it becomes easier for him to understand what should be focused on, that a painting requires a center of interest.

However, if the student has no previous experience, that is good too, because it will be easier for him to adopt the studio ethics; he won't have too many qualms to worry him. In some ways, it can be an ideal advantage favoring you—your mind and talent are raw.

The Offer

My normal routine in teaching is to look at what a student is working on and then point out things that are good and other things that are going wrong. I also point out what will go wrong if some problems aren't addressed and corrected. After that kind of assessment, I give some technical suggestions. If necessary, I work directly on the student's painting to show him how he can solve the problem.

Once, I realized that one of my new students was constantly arguing and asking questions, most of which were unnecessary. At first, I thought she was not aware of how often she asked questions but then I noticed how much she enjoyed "being right." After some weeks, nothing changed and we were still doing the Tango. More time passed and I realized I wasn't too happy with her progress, and she wasn't either. During one class, I asked her to join me outside the studio so we could talk. We were both concerned because she couldn't handle the most basic stuff. After talking, we went back into the studio and I started once more to help her with her painting and, lo and behold, the Tango started again.

After that I tried several different ways to let her know I would rather that I teach and she paint rather than that we both dance. But nothing worked. At this point, the student began to notice that she was enjoying the dance routine, but I was not.

One day after I finished helping another student, my dance partner ran up to me and said she had some questions for me, and that she would be waiting for me outside the room. Imagine an art student waiting with questions for the instructor. Just fifty years ago, she would have been waiting for the Maestro. Being aware that I had been reduced from Maestro to Painting Teacher, I politely responded to her, "I will be there in a minute." She said, "Okay, Sam." A hundred years ago she would have responded, "Thank you Maestro."

When I went to her, I saw that she had a list of questions. As she started reading off the list, I made up my mind to stop the dance, since her failure to learn under my tutelage is a reflection on my teaching.

When she finished reading the list, I said to her, "I'd like to give you the most amazing offer. It is an offer no one has ever refused. It brings the best out of all students, and you will find your work will magically improve. By accepting this offer, your painting skills will develop so much that you will not understand why you never got this offer before." She looked at me, skeptical but intrigued. I asked her what her former profession was. She asked me why I wanted to know. I said I wanted to know so I could judge which offer would best suit her. She said, "I am an attorney. Can't you tell that, Sam?" I responded, "I will now make the offer better than I promised before." She smiled and asked me, "What is the offer?" I said, "Based on the number of students I have, each student deserves my attention for ten to fifteen minutes during each class. But I will give you twenty minutes. I will take the extra five minutes from other students and give it to you." She smiled again. "That's nice," she said. Then I said, "When I come to you, you are entitled to do the talking for twenty minutes and I will listen. Or I will use those twenty minutes to teach you by analyzing your work, showing you technically how to solve problems, and giving you useful advice. I will give you the best of my teaching skills for twenty minutes. Twenty minutes—you do the talking, or I help you. That's my offer." She chose the option where I do the teaching. I said to her, "Everyone chooses that one."

Knowing that reading and researching rhymes very well with attorneys, I encouraged my tango partner to read some inspiring art books, which I had recommended for the class. If she does so, her painting, art history and art appreciation will improve simultaneously.

This story is not a classic example of how students are, or how lawyers behave in painting class. All students by and large are innocent, with no malicious intent. It is just one extreme example I took from many years of teaching. I included it just to illustrate a certain point about attitude, and also to bring to the awareness of the reader that some behaviors can get in the way of learning, and they can slow down the student's progress. If the student is aware of these behavioral problems, then the student will be cautious when dealing with teachers.

Because of my Graphic Arts background, composition has been the easiest subject for me, and the most fun to tackle. I cannot pick up a blank canvas and not worry about what the composition will be. Any student with a business background can gain so much from that experience, likewise a lawyer or a writer. A farmer feels more appreciation for nature than someone from the city. Because of the Noble attitude all artists have, there is no other profession that cannot be helpful to the improvement of the art education.

INVESTING IN YOUR TALENT

(Why Acquire an Art Education?)

You Are What You Know.

To understand the importance of art education is to see education as an invest-ment. Your future achievements are unlimited. You need to get from education all the skills you can to prepare and be ready when opportunities start to arrive.

A student of mine was having difficulties loosening up with his drawing. At first I introduced him to some exercises to free him from being so tight in his work. Nevertheless, for a while, nothing seemed to work. For his particular problem, I real-ized that by copying a certain artist's work, he would learn from that artist. So, I rec-ommended he buy a book about that artist and do some copies of his work, then bring them to class so that I can check the work for him.

The book was about $75. The tuition at the school then was about $850 for a quarter (eight weeks). A month passed by and I realized he still hadn't bought the book and his drawings were still suffering from stiffness. So I asked him about the book. At first, he said he does not like that artist and he can't afford to spend $75 on an artist he does not like. I explained that sometimes knowledge could come from sources that we least expect to provide it. For that same reason the student should not criticize professional artists, but rather look for their strength, and figure out what he can learn from their work. I have become who I am because of all the artists I have studied and who I will become in the future will depend on my life experiences, the works I will see, the books I will read—and that's why open-minded artists can never tell how they will work tomorrow. Besides I don't personally believe in advocating to my students that the tradition we are learning from is the only way. My goal is to con-vince students that, while you might not like an artist's work, you can learn by looking at things you don't want to look at. Also, if history, after 50 to 75 years, has a high regard for a certain artist, he deserves our attention. For learning's sake, the student should accept and respond to scholars.

After giving several reasons, and answering questions, I was sure I had got-ten to the student. After some weeks had passed by, I asked him about the book and the copies. He told me that times are bad and he was unable to afford $75. At this point, I had had it and I saw that I was not going to convince him, so I just said, "I guess your work is not that important to you."

A week later he had gone and bought the book, done about ten copies, and his work had changed. During the following months, his drawings started getting attention from the school. Almost a year passed by, life was good, but then I realized his drawings were, little by little, getting stiff again. At first, he mentioned it but I left it alone, thinking maybe that kind of style is what he psychologically likes. Again, he came in and bitterly complained about how much he really didn't like the stiffness. At this point about a year and a couple of months had passed since I last recommended the book.

I asked him to bring the book to class so that I could explain some technical problems to him. He then said to me, he had sent back the book for a refund two months after he bought it. So, I looked at him and said, "You took the book, learned from it, got some recognition, then sent it back to outsmart the bookstore and get your $75 back! Wow! I was never as smart as you during my student days. I kept my books as reference but lost my money."

At this point, I couldn't help but tell an African story about people who outsmart others. You deceive no one else but yourself. This student was older than me so I didn't have the guts to be direct and chastise him. But I know the class likes to hear my stories, so I decided to tell him a story instead. It is about two friends who deceived the voodoo man.

Two Friends Who Deceived a Voodoo Man

Two friends were recruited into the army. Not long afterwards, they were asked to report for duty. They had to go and fight on the battlefront. The casualties were so bad that these two friends knew it was almost suicidal to go to the war. They decided to consult a voodoo man for magical assistance.

Before the voodoo man could perform the magic that would make them vanish whenever they were in danger, he asked the two friends to bring him two pure white roosters (not a single feather could be of a different color).

After several weeks of searching for the two roosters, one friend found his pure white rooster, but he continued helping his friend to find his rooster. Often, one will have no trouble finding a white rooster, but after looking the rooster over carefully, one sometimes finds a small feather that is not white, a feather the size of a pin, often almost invisible. The two friends realized that the farther away they got from their town the whiter the fowls were getting, so they decided to continue searching. At one point the friend who had found his fowl became tired of the search. After some days and very far from town, they came to a village where all the fowls were white so they bought one. But just before they took it to the medicine man they realized that there was a tiny, tiny, tiny little grey feather between the thighs of the fowl. So they took the rooster back to where they bought it for an exchange.

The poultry farmer said to them that some of the fowls were pure white and several young men had come and bought them. He said he was sure there were more but it would take a while to search and find them. At that point the two friends felt they were too tired to continue the search. So they argued back and forth as to whether they should pluck the tiny feather out. The feather was so pale that no one else would see it anyway. They argued back and forth, and finally through the persuasion of the friend who already had his pure white fowl decided that the voodoo man wouldn't notice it if they plucked out the feather and there was no one to tell on them anyway.

They brought the two white fowls to the voodoo man. The voodoo man performed all the necessary rituals and gave them three words to recite whenever they wanted to vanish. They were to vanish at any danger so long as they recited the three words, even if the enemy were a foot away. After the instructions, the voodoo man told them, "You are free to go. You are now the two fowls I killed. Therefore, you cannot be killed. Go fight and come home successfully."

One day when they were in danger on the battlefield, finding themselves cornered by enemies a couple of yards away, they recited the three words before the enemies shot at them and then they vanished. The enemies were surprised and shocked and looked at each other and began to argue as to whether they had really seen two people because now they couldn't. The enemies gave it up, thinking they were having an hallucination so they decided to sit and rest. After some minutes of resting, one soldier noticed that in between two roots of a tree there was a human (you know what). The astonished soldiers cut off the merchandise. The feather the two friends had plucked was the private parts of one of them. Imagine if they had searched harder and not deceived the voodoo man!

After the story, I added another short African proverb: Whenever you bend down low, peeping at someone's behind, remember there is someone far away peeping at yours too—maybe with a high-definition telescope.

Do not be stingy with your talent. Or outsmart your talent by not buying books. Whatever reference material you buy for your education is a worthwhile investment. Whatever the cost, remember that you are investing in your talent. Everything you do, everything you see, adds to your artistic knowledge and eventually everything will help to make you better, to improve and grow. The way you reason and your thoughts become part of your creative works. Sometimes the bigger the investment, the bigger the rewards. Understand what kind of investment in their education doctors, businessmen, lawyers and architects make—how much time, money, devotion and passion. Great masterpieces created by a few simple strokes are supported by a rich, grand, experienced and knowledgeable mind. Search for knowledge. It is very difficult to put a price on any sort of knowledge and experience in one's field. Knowledge and enrichment of the mind are attainable but not always free, sometimes the price tag is very dear, sometimes not so dear.

THE NOBLE REASONS FOR CHOOSING ART

Pursuit of a Noble Vocation
"Where the spirit does not work with the hand there is no art"
—Leonardo da Vinci

Street Musician
Once on my way home I saw a street musician, a guitarist. In his open guitar box, he displayed coins and dollars so that passersby could throw in donations. In the guitar box, he also has about seven 8x10-inch photographs of great guitarists: Jimi Hendrix, Charlie Christian, Wes Montgomery.

Seeing the lineup of photos of these great guitarists, I sensed an opportunity to learn something, so I threw in a dollar, then waited until his break. "Who is Charlie Christian?" I asked. "Oh my friend, you got to find Charlie Christian, he is your man, the soul man of guitar." After an introduction on the guitar, I got a lecture of about three minutes on Charlie Christian.

"What about Wes Montgomery?" I asked.

"My friend, are you from Africa?" he asked.

"Yes, I am."

"When you think of Soul, when you think of the spiritual qualities that

Figure 18

FRANK DUVENECK, *(American 1848-1919)*

For posters or information, call or visit Cincinnati Art Museum
(513) 639-2995
www.cincinnati artmuseum.org

come out of your music, think of Wes Montgomery," he replied, then he gave me some more minutes of lecture on the evolution of guitar playing from the Thirties to the present time. "They all came from Wes Montgomery," he said, "every guitarist came from Wes Montgomery."

By this time, I had missed five trains, and was running late getting to my studio.   Still, I couldn't help but try to squeeze in one more lesson. So, I tried the Colombo approach.

I innocently asked, "Come on, my friend," I said to him, "Jim is the man, my hero, the lessons you gave me tell me these guys are all great masters in their own right. But let's face it, Jimi Hendrix is still the man."

"They all have the spirit and the soul, that African Soul, and they all lived in different times, and brought their different souls and experiences to their music, the soul that young artists are missing today. The soul that made rhythm and blues so effective," he answered.

For a moment I thought to myself, "How can this guy know so much, play so well, and still play on the streets and in the New York City subway."

I couldn't help behaving like Colombo again. I asked him, "You are so good I wish you had a record out. I would like to buy one—why don't you?"

"It is not all about record deals, nor is it just about being famous," he said. "It is very pleasing to play and entertain people on the street, when they are coming home from work and need some soothing sound to finish their day, it is nice to be around and play for them. It makes being a musician a worthwhile life to live. Raw, natural and directly to the people."

I thought the lesson worth more than a buck so I threw in five bucks, hopped on the train, and started to think how I could share this invaluable metaphysical artistic way of seeing and living life with my students.

If the artist sits for a moment and thinks about the reasons for choosing art as a vocation, he will discover several noble reasons why he wants to become an artist, such as love of nature and love of people, and the most noble reason of all—to make a difference that will improve man's life directly or indirectly, to share what his mind's eye sees and what he internally feels while observing, studying or responding to nature, in hopes that it will better society. The dancer shares inward feelings through the outward movements of his body in hopes that people will feel good about watching him; the writer by the use of words, and the politician by how he helps the public; the philosopher by asking questions and posing answers that will lead to uncovering new ideas. Unfortunately, without a good, realistic, solid knowledge and experience of how to solve technical problems that arise in creating artwork, the artist will not be able to share these beautiful invaluable things with anyone. After all, these ideas all go through several stages before the actual message achieves its goal.

Every great idea shapes the world around it. - Anonymous

One of the amazing rewards in choosing the field of art is the noble realization that the artist's creations can make indirect changes in society, that the artist's work can enrich homes, can bring inspiration to many, and most of all, the artist's creations remind man that men do not live by bread alone. It is for these reasons that some artists never give up their goal of achieving beauty or order. And it is because of the achievements of these artists that our society has developed to this level. Imagine a world without the art that has been created by noble minds.

Regardless of whether we choose to pursue art or art selects us, the extent to which we are able to bring new ways of seeing the world into being will depend on how religious we are about this noble vocation.

Passionate Reasons for Painting
Choose the work you like, and you will never work a day in your life.
- Confucius

Years ago I was in the park; it was winter, about 30 degrees and very windy. My left hand was supporting a canvas and easel while my other hand was painting. A young couple strolling in the park came and stood nearby, watching me struggle. Later, the guy asked me what I planned to do with the painting when I finished it and if there is someone waiting to buy the painting. There is no one waiting for it, I told him, though I might sell it in the future, but I don't know when. He looked at me and looked at his partner and he said to her, "I would not wake up and suffer in this morning cold for anything unless there is a good price attached."

At that moment, I understood the purpose that would make him wake up in the morning to go to work in the freezing cold, but I was driven by a purpose without any price attached. A winter landscape scene. That was the moment in my life when I realized my purpose, it became very clear and I realized that it had not changed at all since my teenage years. I dreamt of becoming an artist in order to portray nature's hidden treasures in a pictorial manner. It was this purpose that drove me from Ghana to Nigeria to Italy and then to New York City, as well as to India and to several other countries in Europe.

There are different purposes that motivate the student or the artist to learn or to create. The measure of the reason or purpose determines how much the student is willing to sacrifice to achieve his goal. It is very important for the artist to continuously remind himself of the reasons why he is pursuing the art as this confirmation keeps the mind focused and makes the artistic life worth living.

What price are we willing to pay to achieve our dreams and pursue our artistic profession? How much do we believe in the purpose behind our creative endeavors? Whether we are willing to sacrifice some years to acquire a good education (or not) depends on how important we feel our purpose is, and how much we want to make a difference in other people's lives.

To some, art is therapeutic; to others, it is a way of communicating or sharing an idea or message. To many, and to the honest, sincere and true artist, art's use is to serve people and better life—to ease life's ever-changing complexities, to open new and better ways of looking at the world.

The importance to us of our ambitions, dreams and goals is what makes us endure the years of sacrifice for our studies. Often the more noble our ambitions and goals are the more enlightened we are and the more we endure. Good thoughts and noble goals make it easier to endure the difficulties that with lesser dreams amount to nothing more than self-indulgence. Noble ambition strengthens our will to get the best education. The more ambitious our dreams, the more time the artist is willing to sacrifice to his studies. So, the student needs to clarify his purpose in choosing the art field and make sure he finds it worth the sacrifice. This does not mean you cannot study without knowing what you want to do with your education. The student can achieve his wishes without having to constantly remind himself of his goals, but it is easier to focus on achieving a certain goal when the student has some definite ideas of what his dreams and ambitions are. The student's dreams and ambitions may change along the way but it is still important, as well as easier and more motivating, if he has a set of goals and reasons, and dreams and ambitions, that are worth the fight.

Students with informed knowledge and prepared minds tend to be more focused on the right things to do and are not as frustrated as those who haven't thought about their future, because they see art as a field that deserves the same preparation and approach as other serious professions and trades, such as law, medicine or business.

The Decision to Choose the Noble Path of Becoming an Artist

One day you wake up and realize you've got some talent, and you love art and want to pursue a career as an artist. The decisions you will make right after that thought will depend on who you are as a person and how you view the study of art. If you are:

a.) A passive person or a dreamer. You will swing around from one studio to another, waiting to be transformed into an artist.
b.) A proactive person, but inactive.
c.) A logic and practical person (realist). You will reason through the process of becoming an artist, and then formulate a practical and logical plan of approach to your goals.

If you are a passive person or a dreamer, chances are you will think any sort of education will be enough, and everything else will be taken care of simply because you worked hard as a student.

If you are a proactive person, but inactive, chances are you will believe in studying, have some education but you believe that your hope of making it to where you wish to go should depend on how hard you work. You will think that your hardworking ethics are what will reward you. Therefore, you will rely a lot on your work ethic.

If you are a logical and practical person, the first thing you will do is make a plan—jot down some thoughts about how you might go about acquiring an education. Ask yourself some questions based on practical and logical reasoning. You might ask yourself:

Figure 19 *The artist Nao Otaka Painting out of doors, Central Park, New York*

- How long will it take to acquire a reliable foundation in the field of art I wish to enter?
- Where can I get a good affordable education?
- What price will I have to pay to become as good an artist as I wish?
- What research do I need to do to find good professional painters who can teach me? And to find a professional painter who can be a mentor to me?
- What else will my education require?
- Should I seek advice from an expert? If so, who?
- Do I have what it takes?

Regarding teaching, the person who is logical and practical will approach the profession the right way, and will therefore be in control of his or her fate. The rest will have to depend on luck. The luck it takes to find the right deal (good and affordable art education). The luck it takes to find the right instructors. And the luck it takes to do everything else such an education requires but that we can't think of at the moment!

Twenty-five years around art students and art enthusiasts has taught me that the artist you will become tomorrow has nothing to do with your talent, or what you have brought to the studio (learning environment). At the end of the day, everyone has some kind of talent. The way you approach art, the attitude you bring to it, is what it is all about. Not just the student who paints well or displays incredible talent will reach the desired destination.

It is not by magic that some artists become good, nor is it by bad luck some never achieve their aims. This book will inform you about some common faults that keep students from realizing the dreams they had before they entered a studio.

Because of some uncertain factors (such as birds, rain, weather), not all butterfly eggs will become caterpillars and not all caterpillars will evolve into beautiful butterflies. But the experts who know more about butterflies tend to have more success raising the insects on butterfly farms than occurs when butterflies lay their eggs in random places. Investing in one's talent cannot solely depend on luck. Even though the butterfly has made a long trip before becoming a butterfly, a bird can still eat it if the butterfly has no knowledge about which zone to fly in.

Full-Time and Part-Time Students

It is possible for the part-time student to acquire great skills, but it is much easier to learn and become an artist if you engage in study full-time rather than part-time. However, don't think that just because you have five days a week over five years to invest in your study that that will guarantee your dream of becoming an artist and surviving in the dog-eat-dog art world. While the amount of time a full-time student gives to his art education does give him an advantage over a part-time student, he will only gain this advantage if he is devoted, loyal, dedicated, hardworking and passionate about learning. Learning art holds no exceptions under the Law of Learning, which rewards only those who are passionate, loyal, devoted and hardworking. Those students, whether they are full-time or part-time learn more in order to know more, in order to succeed because they are willing to honestly invest the mind, the soul, and the body, at any given time, wherever and whenever.

If the student cannot afford full-time study, he should put every ounce of his energy into learning whatever he can. There is an advantage to full-time study, but there is no guarantee of success if the student has no plan, nor any ideas of the right approach to take. If this is the case, studying full-time just allows a student more time to keep searching. Art as a vocation is more generous than other professional fields; in the end result, it does not discriminate between the slow learners and those who catch on fast. Eventually, the full-time student who starts to reason properly will have attained the same level as he who got it in a short time, just as the part-time student who is dedicated and passionate will, with time, be rewarded with the same standing as the full-time student. Anyone who can afford full-time study should count his blessings—it is a great advantage and privilege but it does not mean that the full-time student is better than the part-time student. It is not how many years you put in or how great your talent is. It is how much effort you put in while studying that makes the difference. The rewards you will gain after finishing school will depend on the experience and knowledge you acquire during your school years.

The Gods, the Spirits and Their Rewards

Imagine: How unfair would it be if the Spirits and the Gods had to be partial in the way they treated the souls they have chosen to take care of the physical universe? How could they expect the universe to go on, flourish and live on forever if they themselves are biased and unfair? Should a student be rewarded just because he is charming and has so much talent? Should the devoted, dedicated, hardworking loyal student be punished because he only studies part-time? Why should a student who works intensively for sixteen hours over the weekend after a week of work be rewarded less just because the intensive effort happens on the weekend? Do we become better artists just because we drag our bodies to five days of class each week, while leaving our spirit, minds and thoughts elsewhere? Or do we get better because we show up less often but with all our faculties fully engaged? Total devotion and dedication coupled with full-time study will give full-time students the advantage.

Consider this: The average three-hour life painting class, after all the breaks are subtracted, adds up to only 1 hour and 45 minutes of actual painting time (The model gets six five-minute breaks and one 25-minute break and it takes two minutes to set up the model after each break). This is a total of just under nine class hours a week if a student attends a three-hour class five days a week. It does not sound right to only spend nine hours per week learning a profession that everyone thinks is tough. It is inevitable that there will be too many odds against the student who invests just nine hours a week in any profession. Nine hours a week cannot provide the full experience, knowledge and wisdom to guide any student to success and fortune. The Gods will not hand success and fortune over to such an uncommitted practitioner. And often when a student is in class his mind is outside the studio—I have seen students running at breaks to their newspapers, to take their minds off our intense painting practice. And I have seen students during break putting intense 100% dedication into reading art books or drawing, or solving painting problems that require the model to be there.

The student who paints intensely for about sixteen hours on a weekend is not that different from the student painting nine hours a week for two weeks. The level of intensity makes all the difference.

In learning art, the amount of time you put in can make a big difference, yet it is not always the amount of time invested that guarantees how good you become or how well you learn. It is helpful for a student to consider that it is not the amount of time he puts in but rather how that time is invested, and to think whether just because he puts in so much time, he is entitled to be good. The student who takes weekend or night classes cannot be held back because of his schedule if he is putting in the same level of intensity. It is what the student is learning, and how much effort he is putting forth while in class that makes the difference, not the time. Compare the study of art to the study of law, medicine or business. Compare the artist to a lawyer, a doctor or a businessman. Until art students make these comparisons themselves, and get practical about their studies, taking them as seriously as those of any other profession, they should not expect any special favors or handouts from the Gods when they finish their studies.

Becoming a good artist depends on where you invest your talent, as well as how and when and what you invest your talent in. Your return on your investment will be impacted by the answers to these questions.

What we get in return depends on how devoted, dedicated and passionate we are. Those qualities, supported by a good logical mind, will determine our success.

Figure 20 *Corner of Sam Adoquei's Studio*

CHAPTER ◄O4◄

ATTITUDE AND BEHAVIOR
(Food for Thought)

Some Studio Etiquette to Consider
People will comb your hair according to how you oil it. —African proverb

"How is your work going?" I once asked a student in a painting class.
"What do you mean?" he answered in a deep voice.
"Let me see if I can help you with some input into things that might be going wrong," I continued.
"I like everything and I don't want to change anything," he answered. *"Please Sam, come to me after the break, I am really into my painting."*

Even though this simple five-minute dialogue sounds so innocent and naïve, pushing instructors away is still a damaging message for a student to send.

This chapter is so important and yet so basic that when I started writing it, I got worried that it might be insulting to the intelligence of all those students who are so comfortable to work with. In order to play it safe, I stopped writing it, but before the book went to publication, I changed my mind and decided to take the chance and include it in hopes that students reading this book will see it as a signal to help other students who deserve the best teaching, but might deprive themselves with similar innocent behaviors. The generosity of some kind teachers who helped me brought me here today, and I don't know how I would have learned if not for these instructors' generous, candid and honest approaches to teaching. I am now able to write this book because of the honest and true advice others have given me in the past. People were so honest; they never held back on what they thought was good for me.

The other reason I decided to include this chapter is because it's so easy for attitude problems to hold back an innocent student.

Summarized

What might seem like "kissing up" in a business office—such as the demure obeying of orders, or careful compliance to instructions—can come across in a studio as respectful to the artist and the studio. The same goes for "acting-out" behaviors. Excessive questions in a business environment can be good, an argument with a boss can sometimes be a sign of brainstorming, but in the studio the student has to be careful. Questions and arguments can come across as challenging and can be percieved as disrespectful. At the office or elsewhere, constant questions and challenges of subordinates by an authority figure can come across as picking on someone, or harassment, whereas in the studio, it is always a sign that the instructor wants to push your talent and wants to get the best from you.

Asking Questions

Asking questions is very tricky in a painting class. Some questions may be well meant but can come across as doubtful or challenging. Most professionals, most experienced instructors, and good painters with a good teaching record don't like these sort of questions because they are teaching the basics, and believe that you learn by doing and practicing repeatedly what they want you to do. If they realize you are not getting the lesson, they will explain without your having to ask. They will be ahead of you in anticipating your learning needs. Their programs are often so personalized that you never have to worry; you just work on solving a certain problem. The instructor comes around and analyzes your work, then points out what is to be done. Everything is so basic that the setup incorporates explanations about the methods being taught.

On the other hand, inexperienced teachers will always be ambiguous in the things they teach so, when in doubt, ask as many questions as possible. In all, it is better to ask than worry about something you don't understand. By being cautious and careful your questions will come across well.

THE HUMILITY OF RAPHAEL

The Importance of the Right Attitude

It was said that when Leonardo first met Raphael, Raphael's attitude so impressed him that Leonardo couldn't help but invite Raphael to his private studio to show him the Mona Lisa in progress. And John Singer Sargent was laughed at by other students for being a teacher's pet. As a student, I loved being the teacher's pet. It always made me feel so proud. It never occurred to me to be otherwise—Leonardo himself was like a teacher's pet to Verrocchio. Velázquez's attitude was also impressive and pleasant enough that Rubens did not mind introducing him around and opening up new avenues to him. There are countless successful people that owe their greatness to the masters who never held back their invaluable knowledge and wisdom. These masters knew and continue to know that if the attitude the student displays is good enough, it deserves the best of everything. The masters know that only a noble man at heart can pursue a noble cause and are always willing to share their findings with students or friends who have the trait of nobility.

Sometimes, when I see how some students talk to their instructors and ask questions, it becomes very difficult to tell if the student has the respect worthy of the instructor's best gifts. Often students are too casual or careless with their teachers and this shows a lack of respect. If this buddy-buddy rapport continues, how can the instructor feel comfortable opening up one hundred percent? It is hard to explain how personal and private artists can get with their knowledge and wisdom, and for these reasons tuition and talent are not enough for the student looking to take their art far. Almost all professional artists I have met and my good artist friends credit some of their success to some generous artist who gave them more than they expected. And when you read between the lines of their description of the relationship, you can feel the strong bond between teacher and student in the relationship.

Since my early years at school until now, my motto for learning has always been that once I walk out of my home, studio or school—whatever I am learning and whoever is teaching me are the most important things in my world. It is because of these teachers that I will learn new important things; it is because of these teachers that I might fulfill my dream of the quest to improve myself.

Figure 21 NAO OTAKA, *Bread and Eggs, oil on canvas*

Without that particular learning environment, I would not have anywhere more to go. My teachers have what I need for my future even if I think I can get it somewhere else. My teachers have the right to give me that which I deserve, nothing more and nothing less. Anything that I can do to show my sincere appreciation—my gratitude—I will do. My teachers are my masters whom I enjoy serving, or should enjoy serving.

As a student I have always asked myself: If I were in the shoes of the teacher and the student behaved the way that I do, how much would I give to a student and how far out of my way would I go for that student?

A student will get exactly what he thinks he wants. He will not get that extra attention or instruction that might make all the difference. It is nice to consider, or imagine, that you worked hard all your life to acquire experience, knowledge and wisdom, how you would share that knowledge and wisdom? After all, we are in a noble field and it will not hurt to start cultivating that noble side of your sensibilities.

Kindness, a good attitude, compassion, caring behavior—these are some of the personal qualities that every person likes to be around. Even if they don't think they want to be around people who display these characteristics, chances are they appreciate people who act toward them in this way. Caring for others and being cared for are part of human fulfillment and almost all teachers prefer to give their special knowledge and wisdom to deserving students. One of my older friends from Russia used to tell me, "You know Sam! You're like a brother to me, that's why I can be so demanding of your talent." He was a graduate of one of Russia's most prestigious art academies, the Ilya. Repin St. Petersburg State Academy Institute of Painting, Sculpture and Architecture.

The theory of the baker's dozen is as simple as this: When you paid for your dozen rolls, did you have to ask for that extra one, or did the baker throw in the extra without your asking? Even when you have to ask for the extra, the baker still gets to decide whether to give you a burnt roll or a good one. If he decides to throw in the extra one, he still gets to decide whether to give you fresh bread or fresh bread with butter.

It cannot be underestimated how important it is for students to think a bit about the development of their noble attitude toward the environment they work in and the people they work with. I am convinced that this is the first thing the student should cultivate before entering any studio.

Despite status or age, it would be nice if students would consider cultivating or at least checking their attitude and behavior. It is not part of the official requirement, or the written law of learning but it takes students farther than all the written laws of learning. It can take good students as far as they wish, and even beyond. Without a giving, humble, reverential attitude the student only gets what he paid for. It may not be the same at America's traditional colleges, but in Art Studios, the interaction between students and teachers is more personal and intimate.

Art school is very different from traditional college. As a student develops, he will need to have the opportunity to work closely with the master if he wishes to be provided with some extra intimate experience and be given very honest advice on pursuing art. But before the student can get such an opportunity to

work closely with his master, several things have to be right—talent is the least important ingredient of what is needed.

Looking back through all the years I have spent learning, I credit all that I gained, all that I know, to the lessons that came from my teachers' kindness and generosity. For sure, it was never my talent alone in my college years. At my

Figure 22 (left)

SAMUEL ADOQUEI
*Legacy of Dr. Martin
Luther King, center
panel*

Figure 23 (right)

USHA SHARMA
Untitled

*Courtesy of National
Academy School of
Fine Arts
(212) 996-1908*

art school, only two of us were invited to the private studios of the principal and the head of the school. Even though I cannot pinpoint what exactly made the difference in my growth through these experiences, it is no coincidence that my friend and I after so many years are doing well.

There are countless successful people in all fields whose achievements can be credited not just to their knowledge of the field and their hard work, but to their character and good attitude as well. When we pay attention to our daily engagements with the world around us, we see that people with good character and the right attitude go far. In all the fields that I know of, regarding anything that deals with sharing information or passing on knowledge, it is always character and attitude that win the acceptance of those who have privileges to share.

Figure 24

JOAQUIN BATISDA y SOROLLA

Hispanic Society of America

For posters of Joaquin Sorolla's work, call (212) 926-2234 or visit: www.hispanicsociety.org

CHAPTER ◂O5◂

FINDING THE RIGHT SCHOOL OR TEACHER

Teaching and Learning

What Is Relevant and What Is Irrelevant in a Learning Environment?

"How odd it is for men to grow up in the dark, like mushrooms, ignoring the generation of artists before them. Those who know nothing often think that those who know something stand in their way. On the contrary, they could find guidance from those who know if they but sought it." —Paul Cezanne

One way to make a living as an artist is to teach. What is important in a teaching environment when a student's tuition, time and future are at stake? What is good and important in a teaching environment, and what is irrelevant? What should be the priorities in an art classroom? Whenever tuition, time and future are at stake for the beginner, the most important thing is acquiring the basic skills to build on and that which will help the student continue improving long after school. And the frame of mind needed to find that which might improve the student after school.

Problem-solving solutions that will equip and empower students become the priorities of both the beginner and the teacher. Teachers need to assign projects that help students learn how to acquire skills for professional and survival reasons, as opposed to developing limited styles and habits that don't benefit the aspiring artist in the real world. Because of these ambiguities, students who fail to acquire basic skills will always pay the greatest price, both in tuition and in years dedicated to their studies.

These are among the reasons why well prepared and well informed students will want to know what is important to learn in a studio, as well as what to expect and what to avoid. Among these issues are: not knowing the difference between the science of art and the art itself; knowing the difference between an artist and a student; and also how to differentiate between an artist who is well grounded, skillful and experienced and an artist who is talented and creative. An artist can be creative and talented but not skillful; creativity and talent are things that most students have an abundance of. Therefore, they are not the most important qualities to have.

Before Enrolling in any Art School

Even though a student at first might be drawn to a certain style, an informed student needs to remember to suppress his or her likings to avoid learning unnecessary skills. Students must be aware that one can learn something, and if that which the student has learned is a style, it is difficult to get it out of one's system. Styles become habits and habitual practices can form the artist within. Students need to know the difference between a style, a traditional approach and a personal approach. If a knowledgeable student takes a practical or logical approach, that will make it easier for the student to know if he or she is in the right environment and learning the right way.

Thus a student will understand that certain projects and exercises were designed for progressive growth and that the projects will not suppress a student's talent, but rather will bring him freedom by allowing the student to use his materials effectively. A well-informed student will also be aware that his instruction time is arranged to achieve progressive results, according to priority. This awareness will prevent him from feeling panicked, or lost. Working on the special subjects set up for learning special lessons are more important than painting whatever the student wants to paint.

At the very least, a student should know the difference between therapeutic art (you create or paint only for personal reasons, such as fun, to be creative or to experiment) and art as a religion or a lifestyle.

The student with a well-prepared approach to learning will always find what he is looking for. All art studios have specific things to offer and the ready and able student will gain at least something, perhaps something different from what he initially expected or what he came in for. For the student to have this experience he has to have some idea of that which he came for. Know that most instructors are professionals in a certain branch of the field, so the prepared student, no matter what the situation, will always gain.

Even though art can be a way of life for most of us, sometimes it can also be therapeutic, a way to make money or just to pass the time. A studio space for teaching could be just a studio space for advanced students to practice and hone their skills or to learn simple new skills; it is still important for the student to be aware of either practicing in order to secure a certain technique or to learn new stuff. I have seen students do everything to improve their work, when in fact, their attitude in class resembles that of persons who want to relax. Sometimes students think that just by being in class they will improve so no need to make that extra effort demanded by a demanding instructor. Most students by and large mean well but because they are uninformed, they do not get a proper return on the years they invest in learning. An informed student knows it is more important to be practicing a method he has not yet mastered and engaging in a specific project to master that method instead of doing his own self-satisfying art work.

As the supply of teachers increases so will the field of teaching. The opportunities to find several qualified teachers will also increase, and they will be available for the well prepared student. One who knows what to look for in a teacher will have more choices than in the past. Students will find it easy to spot the real, honest, qualified, true teachers who don't just charm students. It is hard for real, honest, qualified, true teachers to find students.

Choosing Instructors

There are so many good professional instructors that the student doesn't have to worry about finding one. Professional instructors have a curriculum that focuses on the art and science of creating the craft, the basics of creating and the methodology of the field. In the beginning of a student's career, these are more important than the art of the field. All good instructors have a very good background in the field and are masters of the craft of painting. The student can tell by the amount of hands-on teaching the instructor provides.

It is your life and your future, so it is important to choose your teachers wisely by doing careful research in whatever way is necessary and in recent times the Internet is quite appropriate. It is, therefore, the first place where you might want to start your search for instructors. Any other source, such as a portfolio or one or two reproduced prints, will not be complete enough. Sometimes other sources are filtered through a second or third person. On the Internet, professional artists are likely to show you a complete portfolio, from sketches (including drawings and oil sketches and color studies) to finished works as well as early projects and, in addition, give you some idea of his or her artistic philosophy. The artist's background may also be represented by a posting of his curriculum vitae.

Students today have many more choices in choosing instructors than ever before because they can take advantage of modern technology to access samples of the teacher's artwork—easily looking at the works on the Internet with very little research. When searching for suitable and qualified instructors, the student should always be wary of painters who display only a few works online.

It is best if the student can see works by the instructor that have been completed within a span of ten to fifteen years. More than fifteen works done within a period of ten to fifteen years can tell a lot about what the instructor knows and what the student will be learning.

One of the few things that have improved over the years is the opportunity for people of every age group and from every walk of life to have the same access to education. The change often brings challenges to young students who find themselves working next to students who are their mother's or father's age, or even their grandmother's or grandfather's age. The same goes for older, more mature students. They find themselves being challenged by the enthusiasm of the younger students; this situation often helps students with a positive attitude to feed on each other's energy. Given the choice I would rather have this kind of environment than any other. The student is advised to see the value of the situation and enjoy it.

Often a total beginner will find himself in a very intimidating environment, being sandwiched between advanced students, or in the reverse case, an advanced student will be stuck in the midst of total beginners. Such situations test both parties' endurance and temperament, being intimidated by an advanced student or feeling too important around beginners are some of the vices incompatible with learning successfully. At the end of the day, what is important is what the student can get from the studio.

In learning art, there are a number of characteristics that the student and the teacher bring to the learning environment: character, talent and taste are the most common and the most important. Because of these attributes, a student might work well in one teacher's studio, and the same student might feel uncomfortable being taught by another teacher.

An instructor might find it very exciting helping one student while he will not feel enthusiastic in helping another. He can find it interesting and challenging to bring out the best

Figure 25 SAMUEL ADOQUEI, *White Silk Kimono*

of the talent of a particular student but not feel the same with another. It does not matter what level the student is at or how great the teacher's teaching skills. Even the teacher who has enough experience to teach almost anyone will every now and then encounter difficult situations. A student might have all the humility needed to work under or with anyone yet he might feel wrong or uncomfortable in a certain artistic environment. This situation has got nothing to do with good or bad character on either side nor has it to do with skill. It is just that some people connect better with each other than with others. There are neither bad teachers nor good teachers. The same applies to students; there are not good or bad students.

The complexities of art make for chemistry and the trust and character between teacher and student is an important factor. Unlike other fields, where chemistry between teacher and student doesn't play an important role, in teaching and learning art, character, chemistry and the trust between teacher and student are very important factors.

Depending on how an individual student performs, he or she might spend two to ten years acquiring sufficient skills and knowledge to pursue an artistic vocation.

It is because of this (plus the large sum of tuition involved and the growth all artists desire to have after school). The message of this book brings new and helpful ways to approach learning; no, this book will not have been necessary, neither will I find it interesting to write it. Art is too personal and learning it varies so much that without time, tuition and growth, the study of art is too abstract and should be left to the individual artist's personal exploration in the hope that the experience an artist gathers in the journey of searching for personal reasons of that individual's life is part of the adventure of being an artist. But this is not the case, an artist might waste too much time, struggling unnecessarily, and yet growth and progress will not come his way. All for simply not giving careful consideration to the field's seriousness and to the planning of how to pursue an education in art. This is the source of inspiration for this book; hopefully the book's message can help those who read it.

If by reading this book the students saves himself a year, or even two or three years, graduating two years earlier than he would otherwise because of the book's advice, it will be worth the read. Two to three years of anyone's life or tuition is too important to waste.

STUDYING WITH DIFFERENT INSTRUCTORS

You are one entity with a unique genetic makeup;
you cannot be everyone.

Michelangelo, Van Gogh and Cézanne saw nature in a sculptural manner. Gauguin, Ingres and a few others saw nature in a smooth, flat and quiet manner. How do you see the world and what suits your temperament? It is hard to know what you like when you are a student and it is best not to worry too much about your preferences; such worries will get in the way of what is important.

In the movie, Lust for Life, Gauguin, in a rage, shouted at Van Gogh that he sees nature as too rough and too rigid and that life is very smooth and flat and the surface of a canvas should be smooth and flat to represent life. Van Gogh, in response, told Gauguin that he sees life as too smooth and too flat and needs to add some roughness. Imagine a student studying with Gauguin and Van Gogh at the same time. Titian, even though he sometimes worked rapidly, is known for glazing a canvas over forty times. Even though Sargent also glazes sometimes, he is better known for his alla prima approach to painting. Ingres, on the other hand, is known for his meticulous planning before starting a painting. Imagine a student studying with Sargent and Ingres at the same time.

Just because several good teachers are available does not mean that the student should try all of them at the same time. Can you imagine a student of Picasso studying under Manet; imagine a student of Sargent studying with Matisse at the same time; imagine the student of Leonardo studying with Michelangelo.

Students should be careful about learning opposing, conflicting, incompatible techniques. Just because two, or three, or even five instructors are good does not mean that what they are teaching will be compatible. The temperament that it takes to solve the problems of one technique might be very different from that needed for another technique. For example, the temperament it takes to stand in front of a life model or landscape and paint rapidly and spontaneously, is very different from the temperament that requires careful preparation—the gathering of information beforehand, followed by planning the work and then working the plan. The differences between Cézanne and Sargent are due to attitude, temperament, personal training, taste, experience and, often, background. Cézanne sees life as a mosaic, a patchy arrangement of color. Sargent organizes what he sees—his arrangements unify into a pleasing whole. Matisse arranges the elements in his paintings to form a strong decorative whole and whatever has to be sacrificed to achieve this goal will be sacrificed.

David and Ingres love to hang onto old traditions while Sargent deals with the times he lives in and realistic things. Courbert and Sorolla also deal with the issues and subjects of their times. Matisse and Picasso deal with the modern and innovative; beauty is redefined by them, it becomes something we never thought of before, something we are not programmed to recognize. What David

Figure 26

SAMUEL
ADOQUEI,
*Portrait of a
Yound Black Girl,*
oil on canvas

and Ingres might find beautiful, Courbet is likely to ignore, and what Courbet would spend months exploring, Ingres would not even want to acknowledge. So does the twentieth-first-century painter throw all of the past away and only look forward? All of these historical artists have philosophical arguments to support their aesthetic. This is too much to think about for a student who just wants to understand the craft in order to have freedom to solve complicated artistic problems in the future. Every artist has his own personal reasons for pursuing art. Some of the reasons are influenced by metaphysical ideas, some by philosophical reasons, others by religion, and some by practical considerations.

Some artists like to repeat or preserve the past. Some like to learn from the past while others want to learn to use past legacies in order to better understand the present, and maybe project it into the future. To some artists, only one thing matters—the present; the past is gone and the future is unknown. How to better live today through art is their only concern. How do we better serve the public in an artistic way? Let your whole being influence your work—your personality, your character, your temperament, your philosophical ideas. In letting all of these qualities honestly influence your work, you cannot go wrong in your pursuit of creating works that are meaningful to mankind.

Because of the modern idea that new and different is better, a beautiful painting in the midst of ugly paintings will look out of place but an ugly painting will look special and unique on a wall among good paintings.

*Ugly paintings look special and unique
in the midst of great paintings.*

For some artists, the past and the present give us a better understanding of what the future can be; therefore they create to let people know what the future might look like, or to prepare the present for the future. Thus indirectly the thoughts and ideas we have today shape tomorrow.

These are among the reasons why almost all artists will teach differently and the differences are very good but being taught by more than one artist is not necessarily compatible with the goals of a student who needs to concentrate on a simple, methodical and scientific technique. A certain metaphysical, philosophical, religious or practical approach might be good for an individual artist as he personally pursues his artistic dreams, yet the same approach might be very confusing to a student who is applying more than one idea at the same time to his education.

Ingres might have literally expected his students to preserve beauty through Greek ideology, while Courbet, Monet and Van Gogh waited for nature to provide them with beauty, ideas and inspirations. On the other hand, Picasso said, "Forget the Old Masters. Let's go to Africa." A twentieth-first-century artist might say, "Society is bad. It's me, me, me! Life is so bad! My therapist wants me to put my feelings onto the canvases and choke everyone with my problems. I want the government to pay for all my responsibilities. Me, me, me! Life is bad, I want to have more cellular phones!" So art becomes therapy. These differences in viewpoint are good for art and interesting for practicing artists, but at the end of the day, a new student just wants to learn technical rules for solving problems so that he too can be equipped to pursue his personal vision and ideas with ease. A student has to have command over the medium before he can easily explore and find his artist-self. Without an understanding of technique and the field, a student will have a hard and frustrating time because he has no control over the materials he uses for what he or she dreams of creating.

While techniques can be confusing, we can't reinvent the wheel. The basics are still the same. After all it is the grammar that the student is learning. While in drawing there are several styles, approaches and methods, there is a proven traditional method that works for almost everyone. A complete understanding of this method allows the artist to find his or her own style of working. In painting, a student has to learn about values, forms and color, and in drawing, a student has to learn construction, light and shade, form, etc.

THE GRAMMAR OF LEARNING

The prepared student will need to differentiate between the art and science of art. He will need to learn the difference between an art student and an artist, between what a student wants and what is necessary for a student or what is good for a student at a certain stage in his education. After understanding these elements, an artist will find it easy to work in the more personal styles of drawing or painting, such as contour, gesture, inside-out and outside-in.

As I explained, artists teach for several reasons, and often not because they know the ins and outs of the field and perhaps not because they want to give

Figure 27 SAMUEL ADOQUEI, *Untitled, oil on canvas*

back. A student could study with an artist who teaches styles instead of the basics and a student would have no idea of what he was missing.

Know what you want—if art is just a hobby to you, you will do well in a more casual environment.

Look at works by artists who teach before you start to see if their work sets forth the direction you eventually want to go.

Do some homework—inquire who is the best artist and contact that person.

Does he or she teach? Can he or she act as a mentor?

Make sure to stay with the artist you admire, and whose style you would not mind emulating, if you indeed find that person. Give yourself some time to explore the experience of working under him.

Writers do not need to know the whole dictionary in order to write something meaningful that adds to man's life, so likewise, artists do not have to have the skill of the gods. As the saying goes there are three colors in the rainbow, 10 mathematical digits, 26 letters of the alphabet and seven musical notes. It is what you do with them that counts.

Be very careful regarding what you hear from other students, because a student's personal experience sometimes reflects someone else's negative opinion or attitude about a good artist-teacher. I have seen students rapidly improving and progressing, starting from nowhere and becoming very good within a couple of months, when all of a sudden, out of nowhere and because, out of curiosity, they listened to a fellow student who has been a professional student for years. He who was improving got derailed and adopted the habit of hopping from one studio to another. It is wise to be cautious about who you take advice from. Be sensitive and philosophical about advice.

Art schools are full of frustrated professional students who are willing to drag down innocent students—these professional students know it all. They know so much that they have become professional students. However, behavior that is good for Jack might not be good for Cynthia, so use your own logical analysis; when in doubt, listen to your heart, you cannot be that wrong and if you are wrong it is much easier to correct yourself than to straighten out after being pushed by others. When you find someone that you work well with, listen to yourself. Take as much as you can until your heart tells you otherwise. If possible go in with an open mind and have your own experience. Not all personalities are compatible, one student might be madly in love with the way an instructor teaches while another dislikes that same way. There are several reasons why people study art, from therapeutic to passing time, from trying out one's talent to improving one's talent. From brushing up one's skills to searching for a career.

Your life and reasons and goals are never the same as those of the student painting next to you, or the one who is telling you what to do. You might work very well with one instructor while a friend of yours might not. At the end of the day it is your life, not your friend's, so follow your heart. A student can have a strong personal vendetta against an instructor, and can portray that instructor in a bad light. The instructor can come across as so horrible that you wonder how and why the instructor has students.

At the end of the day it is your life on the line, don't allow your eagerness to be swayed from your goal or your mind to be poisoned. I once read about an instructor who advised in his writings that students who have had bad experiences with a teacher should be sure to discourage any other student who wants to work with that instructor. Imagine someone advocating this behavior. Imagine if all instructors had to behave like lambs in order to keep students. The students wouldn't learn anything. Because of this, be cautious when choosing instructors. I used to recommend that some of my students brush up their skills with other instructors, but over time, I realized that most of the students I had suggested this to never came back. It took some years to realize what was going on. The best thing is to have your own experience with an instructor you admire. It is your time, your investment and your own experience.

Even if you want to become a modern abstract artist, I would not suggest you start your studies with abstract principles. From a technical craft/problem-solving standpoint, in my own personal opinion and through my experience of teaching and seeing the progress of students, the abstract principles are too limiting and philosophical for a student who is supposed to be developing his problem-solving abilities. Almost all good modern artists come from a strong traditional background.

When looking for an instructor, always be sure to view more than 15 works by that person. If an artist does not have more than 10 works of art to show, he is being too cautious. An artist who shows work that spans 10 to15 years gives you an idea of his or her growth and what he or she is capable of doing. An artist with very few works to display will have an advantage over the artist with lots of works on display because, within a period of two to three years, he can have copied some interesting photographs and come up with a couple of strong, attractive works. This is a strategy that might work when hunting for a gallery. However, more than 15 works are needed to truly represent the artist. If you find yourself wanting to study under an artist without a full range of works, then expect to be taught methods based on simple logic. A simple basic methodical hands-on approach is a skill students can build on. Always avoid styles, tricks or gimmicks. It is fun to accept what the instructor has shown and expect to be taught.

THE IMPORTANCE OF HAVING A MENTOR

After deciding to become an artist, you have enrolled in a good atelier or art school or are working privately in an artist's studio, where you are studying all you can in order to be able to begin a lucrative vocation. Is it still necessary to have a mentor? The answer depends on your ambitions.

Imagine, for instance, having a kind and generous friend who makes himself available to you whenever you are in need of a consultation. Imagine an understanding friend who out of kindness and compassion is willing to hand you the secret keys to success in your artistic vocation, someone with the knowledge and wisdom you need, knowledge and wisdom that are not included in the studio or school's curriculum. This sympathetic person, who is connected to the art world, will help you achieve that knowledge and wisdom just for the sake of helping you. On the other hand, imagine being on your own, struggling and searching for answers to your questions, imagine how much work it will take to discover the extra knowledge and wisdom that usually only comes from years of experience. This is why pursuing a vocation is much easier when guided by a mentor than it is without one. With a mentor, that extra knowledge and wisdom come in quick and easy doses; without one, they will come with a heavy price tag. Mentors do not get paid, they help out of sympathy and empathy, and the only reward they get is the good feeling that helping gives them.

The most effective approach to finding a mentor is first to enroll in a workshop taught by a master. In a studio or workshop, it is much easier to prove your sincerity, loyalty and humility. It is also easier to study with and get to know the master before approaching him for the mentorship opportunity. Close contact in a class also helps you gain first-hand knowledge of the mentor's character.

Magazine articles and interviews, as well as school catalogs, are also very helpful in doing research about professional artists and their backgrounds, beliefs, ideas and philosophies. The appropriate way to approach such artists is to send them a sincere and honest letter or email. A more formal approach to finding a mentor is through recommendation by a respectful person acting on your behalf.

When all goes well and the master accepts him, the student will not have to ask the mentor for what he wants. Mentors are aware of the goals of hardwork-

Figure 28

TOM VENTERELLI,
*The Maestro at his
studio, photograph*

*Mr. Venterelli is one
of the leading experts
in Louis Comfort
Tiffany Stained Glass.
Mr. Venterelli has
trained several
stained glass artists.*

ing students, they know you have gravitated towards them because you want to do better and learn more than you can in your current situation. You are hungry for more advice, hungry for ideas, hungry for knowledge, experience and guidance.

It is not what the student wants from the mentor or how talented the student is that impresses the mentor so that he wants to help the student—it is the student's attitude and the impression he gives of humility, sincerity and willingness to work that will impress the mentor.

The relationship between a mentor and his protégé is built solely on trust. The relationship starts off as an adviser and student relationship, it then continues to friendship and ends up being like a family relationship. When this bond is formed, the mentor will do whatever it takes to make sure the student gets the best of whatever he wants. It is this that makes good mentors so important. They give so much for so little in return.

Mentors often test students in order to know if they can work with them. They will test the student's attitude, obedience, humility and will to work. They cannot bestow their friendship and reputation on a stranger who lacks character and humility.

This kind of testing is common with leaders—those who have a lot to lose practice it; their independence, reputation, privacy and profession are at stake. Leaders try several unusual tricks in order to uncover the true character of their followers. They know by experience that circumstances and situations do not make people, but circumstances and situations reveal the true and hidden character of a person. A humble, sincere and loyal student will remain so, no matter what the circumstances are.

How Do You Know When You Have Found the Right Mentor?

Mentors should be professional artists with a broad traditional foundation, but be cautious because not all professional artists have a good enough foundation to be of help to a student in need of the right and proper guidance.

All good mentors possess similar traits—they are generous with their time, they make you feel comfortable enough that you are never afraid or intimidated to approach them with problems and they have no time limit on helping. Such individuals become true and sincere friends who understand your needs. A student may miss the opportunity to recognize a mentor because in a perfect studio environment, the student might take a good teacher's kindness for granted, thinking the extra help and extra effort the teacher provides is part of the curriculum, and therefore the service will always be there. When you find someone whom you think is the right person, look for an opportunity to set up a meeting to discuss your desire to have him as your mentor.

In some fields, it is a common practice for a student to study with one teacher and have a different person as a mentor. In the arts, the best situation is to have your teacher as your mentor, but often situations and conditions in modern life prevent this from happening, forcing a student to have a mentor other than his teacher. If this happens, the student should be very cautious. Art is too complex and the philosophies, ideas and beliefs of artists are too unique to have your ship captained by two captains with different compasses going to separate places.

Figure 29 The Author at 15 painting a billboard, photograph

When Do You Leave Your Mentor?

In time, mentors become like friends or family that you hope to have a last-ing relationship with, so naturally you will always hope to have the relationship with the mentor but you might not always need the same help or the same attention and encouragement as time goes by. A sincere friendship develops and evolves. Mentors are not people you find, hang around with when you need their help, suck their energy from, and then drop. If this happens, the student will not be hurting anyone but himself. It is best not to make a conscious deci-sion to leave your mentor just because you think you have become as good as you wish. In some cultures it is very bad karma to leave a mentor on a bad note. Leonardo da Vinci went back and forth to his master's studio long after he had become a professional artist. Raphael was a good friend to Pietro Perugino, his teacher; it was through Perugino that the young Raphael got to know da Vinci. In the history of great artists and how they achieved their greatness, there are countless masters who kept going back to their teachers/mentors until life decided otherwise. It is a common practice among all great artists. Traditionally, the evolution of great artists is, first, that the artists acquire train-ing, and then they develop, get busy, explore, evolve and become independent.

Good mentors sacrifice a lot and do their best to make sure the student suc-

Figure 30 LISA DINHOFER, *Insects In and Out*

ceeds. After all, they have done everything for no fee. This mentorship relation is an extension of the Mentor's ideas and accomplishments, so it is in the interest of the mentor that the student succeeds. When you start to feel you have learned enough and can move on, move on gracefully and avoid burning the bridge behind you—there may be unexpected storms and floods to come, and also for the sake of others who will cross the bridge. When it comes to the relationship between a mentor and a student it is very wise for the student to try as hard as he can to fix any little damages that may have occurred to the bridge, either during the time he was on the bridge or after crossing.

CHAPTER ◂06◂

THE IMPORTANCE OF SKILL

Technique, Style and Your Artistic Vision

The Ying and Yang of Art

No matter how simple a subject or a creative idea, it can be painted wrong. But with a good plan, any ambitious idea can be executed easily and successfully. The student will enjoy great success if he learns to plan every work. Freedom to paint well that which our heart desires to express is the reason we acquire skill.

How Well Equipped Is Your Creative Toolbox?

How well the artist paints, how easily he solves technical and creative problems and creates depends on his knowledge, experience and understanding of the art and science of his craft.

The student must gain a realistic knowledge of the art and craft of painting through understanding these seven important principles of the art and craft of creating:

• Imitating nature through drawing and painting
• Understanding composition and design
• Using color objectively
• Understanding the materials of the trade
• Developing taste in order to be able to tell good from bad
• Understanding the technical handling of space, motion and atmosphere
• Studying nature constantly in order to continue growing as an artist

Figure 31 *(left)*

SAMUEL
ADOQUEI,
Portrait of Dee

Figure 32 *(right)*

*Portrait in Green,
Painted in Alla prima
technique*

Figure 33
(below far right)

JEANETTE
CHRISTJANSEN,
Cup Cakes

*Painted in thin layers
of paint, similar to
the glazing technique.
Some areas are
painted in the
classical old master
glazing technic.*

The student must also, in the beginning, even if it turns out to be hard to learn, try everything. It is not easy to know what will extract the best from him until he tries everything, exploring all the genres: Portraiture; Figuration (figurative art develops the analytical, mathematical and scientific senses); Still Life (still life develops the technical senses, such as those for understanding texture); Landscape (landscape develops the sense of freedom, of taking chances and not worrying too much about technique and also helps develop a broad habit of unifying and simplifying).

My professional artistic and teaching background makes it easy to know the joy, freedom and power artists with skill have. Yet I will be the first to say that skill is not the only or even the most important asset in pursuing art. The student should make every effort to get as much skill as he/she can by affording the best education if possible but if by chance the student finds it difficult learning to be skillful—no big deal. The student should know that many artists have created wonderful things with very little skill. While many of those artists with the best skills have left us with no traces of their existence. Skill is one of the important factors in making art or in getting your message across, but it is not everything. As Leonardo da Vinci put it, skill is like the oil we put in a vehicle, it makes the vehicle faster.

Personal vision, imagination, freedom and purpose, supported by tremendous skill, are what students need in order to pursue a genuine and successful dream as an artist. The imaginative mind that asks questions and tries to find answers will need to have skill.

So will the visionary who is dissatisfied with the status quo. The free and visionary artist wants to explore. Give this mind a toolbox with some basic

skills in solving general problems and the world will see one more unique entity, with an original voice and a new vision. But take the problem solving equip-
ment away from this talent or take the toolbox away from this inquisitive artistic mind, don't allow this creative inquisitive mind (talent) to gain access to
basic education; deny this mind the stimuli it needs and you will have a frustrated, incapable, discontented creature, his ambitions buried.

Education does not make, break or decide for artists who have that natural
innate vision but rather gives them boundless choices with a toolbox attached.
Therefore, any artist with a will to pursue art seriously should first try to
acquire problem-solving training (the toolbox) that is general and complete,
just so that the mind with big dreams and vision can spend its valuable time
working on important creative ideas, not on solving technical problems.

Students do get attracted to some sort of style; I was no exception. During
my student days, whenever I saw any great master at his best, all I wanted to do
was to paint exactly like that master. Like me new students don't understand
what personal style is all about.

Beginners don't realize how dangerous it is to attempt to adopt someone
else's style and try to do it as well as the originator. They don't realize how
important it is to just concentrate on the basics. Or how easy it will be to develop one's own style after one has mastered the basics.

The artist can create beautifully with just raw talent and without too much
skill, but with skill and command over the medium the artist can easily take on
projects, commissions and deliver without hassle.

The more important our message is, the more accurate the plan should be.

THE IMPORTANCE OF TECHNIQUE

*"Great things are not done by impulse but by a series of small things brought
together."—Vincent van Gogh*

The more you paint the more you run into the same mistakes and the
easier it becomes for you to deal with those mistakes and solve the problems
they present. Every experience on the canvas becomes familiar with time.

In a broader way, the worth of a student is what he knows, what he learns
at school, what he can do, how he sees nature, and his vision. As students these
areas of art are those meant to be developed and improved on.

Technique is the way in which an artist solves problems so that his message can be clearly understood and at the same time hit its target. The growth of an artist goes through the stages of student years, experimental period and mature period. All these periods have their own particular importance and worries.

Figure 34

USHA SHARMA,
Central Park

Figure 35 FRANK WESTON BENSON (1862-1951), *Four Children at North Haven, c. 1903-4, oil on canvas*
Courtesy of Adelson Galleries, New York

CHAPTER ◄07◄

CAN EDUCATION GET IN THE WAY OF CREATIVITY?

Often those who do not understand or know the field think technique gets in the way of creativity. Thinking that might not matter if what the artist has to say is not important, but if what the artist's mind's eye sees is important, then the artist can't afford to say the wrong thing because of technical inefficiencies. Lack of technical skills can force the incompetent artist to settle for that which comes to him by accident, not that which he wants and sees in his mind's eye. Technique is the only vehicle that equips the artist with the freedom to do as he wishes and express on the canvas exactly what the mind's eye sees and what his imagination envisions.

In a broader way the worth of a student is his experience, what he can do, his goals and visions. These are the areas he has to work hard to develop in school.

A beginning businessman who is guided by a successful and wealthy businessman, will not make too many mistakes and will have an easier time of it in his work. A classic example is the Donald Trump T.V. Show, The Apprentice. Those who apply to Trump to be apprentices are educated and successful in their own right, but they still lack the true street-smart intelligence to make it to the top, and for that they seek Trump's ideas and wisdom.

The only reason to study with a professional artist is the need for the beginner to learn the skills needed to solve and handle technical problems so that his worries will be limited to abstract or imaginative ideas.

The art and craft of painting is very simple and easy to learn if it is introduced to the beginner in a simplified step-by-step manner. Because of people's inherently different characteristics, all art students cannot approach the learning of art in the same way; one method can work well with one student but not with another. Technique might be taught the same way but could be introduced differently. For example, two students who are starting to learn art at the same time with the same instructor might not do the same exercises. Technique is like a language; it has its simple basic grammatical structure. The structure can be learned and understood by art students but it will not necessarily be liked by all art students. One student can start learning by describing an apple in pencil while another will start by drawing in charcoal. The more the student understands the importance of the underlying structure the easier it will be for him to use it to communicate or to express himself in conveying his particular idea or message. Students and those who might not fully understand the language of art will fail to communicate their important ideas.

In the struggle to make his ideas or message understood, the student without good skills or understanding of technique finds that agony and frustration awaits him. The experienced student with the confidence of knowing how much he understands the art and craft of painting can give himself some freedom and confidently take on projects he can successfully tackle. On the other hand, the student without confidence regarding what he knows about the art and science of painting is forced to avoid taking on important projects or commissions.

The creativity, dreams and ambitions of a student do not all depend on his level of understanding of the science of creating; skills and technique provide answers to complex technical problems and sometimes ambitious projects.

Our past experiences, our expectations and our different backgrounds can all affect our learning. It is very important that all students prepare themselves well before taking art classes. It is different in other professional fields, in most fields the student's diploma or degree determines how he will perform. Sometimes our differences can make things easy or difficult, depending on how we take advantage of our past experience. Awareness of who we are can make it easy to prepare for the task ahead—the learning process or the artistic journey.

A sixty-year-old who has just begun to study art has to consciously put some unfavorable habits aside in order to make room for new student habits. A twenty-year-old has to control his enthusiasm or insecurities if he wishes to secure a solid foundation or else he will run around in circles trying everything and not mastering the necessary lessons a studio has to offer. The more the student sees technique as a language then the more easily he can focus on the type of language that suits his temperament and that he would like to communicate with.

The decision to choose one artistic language is always determined by who

Figure 36

SAMUEL ADOQUEI,
*Portrait of Sherry
Donnovan,*
oil on canvas

is speaking and to whom the message is directed. Whether he chooses to use an Old Master approach to painting or some other approach that most of today's people understand or, on the other hand, an approach understood only by a selected few is left to the artist. Personally, I prefer speaking to a broader audience. I am more interested in the message I want to share than in what my tone or accent is. In painting it is more important for the viewer to get the message than to understand the technique or style.

So many styles, techniques and methods have been practiced by successful great artists that to recommend one sort of style of working would be hypocritical. I paint the way I do because I whole-heartedly love and believe in everything about the technique and style in which I paint. I love the style passionately as well as the philosophy and reasons it embraces. So do my peers love their technique and style passionately. They might have reasons total differently from mine, which I am sure would make a lot of sense if one knew where they were coming from. Just because I do what I do does not mean my way of working is the only way. Whether he aims to be classical, impressionistic, modern or realistic in style, the artist will still have to learn the art of making images on a two-dimensional surface so that the painting reads well for the viewer. A portrait painting, whether by Raphael, Sargent, Cézanne or Monet has to read, and the same goes for a figure or a still life. The grammar is the same. A sphere has to read like a sphere, a cube like a cube. The artist will deal in the same manner with such concepts as concave, convex, sphere and cube. Understanding space, atmosphere, mood and creating the illusion of these objects or effects on a two-dimensional surface are the reasons for learning the science of creating, and why nature must be reduced down to the level of the materials the artist will be using. Learning to handle and create these illusions is why we go to school. It is their time in history as well as art's evolution and inventions that produced Monet, Picasso and other revolutionaries. Monet couldn't have come 400 years earlier or Michelangelo 400 years later. We face the same fate, for we live in today's world. Not yesterday and not tomorrow.

I have often wondered what Leonardo, Raphael or Rubens would think if one were to show them a painting by Monet or by Vincent van Gogh. How would they respond to the technique and the use of pigment by these artists? Who will time favor the most: Monet, Hokusai, Rubens, Leonardo, Picasso or Cézanne? Or perhaps an African artist? There is no one way of solving technical problems; there is one grammar, but not one way of handling or using the grammar. That grammar is used to create the illusion of three dimensions on a two-dimensional surface.

Students naturally differ in their temperaments, likes and dislikes, yet the same grammatical foundation that worked for these artists (that of being able to draw well and to create a three-dimensional illusion on a two-dimensional surface) guarantees that all students will eventually find their own unique and beautiful way of solving technical problems. No one fails. Everyone at the end masters a way of solving and handling problems. Even babies on their own can find ways to communicate eventually. But it is only with assistance that students learn to express themselves vividly and with practice master their language.

Freedom to Solve Technical Problems

Until he can consistently reproduce a certain predictable result using the same method, and that method has become like a second language, the student will find it difficult to work with freedom in solving technical problems. Painting Technique is a craft and has to be repeated often in order for the student to master it. It takes a short time to learn and understand the craft but it actually takes years to master. It is because of this that art students who are patient and who know the importance of acquiring skills tend to master them before graduating. But it is also because of this that all students, after leaving school or graduating, still go on improving and gaining confidence to tackle difficult projects and assignments.

In all fields, the strongest backbone that supports professionals is their command over the language—their mastery of craft, or technique. It is this mastery of grammar, syntax and vocabulary—the basics—that gives professionals the ability to express what is in their imaginations and to solve problems precisely. It is the same with painting—all the geniuses of the field solve technical problems without ever worrying. This does not mean that without mastery of technique the artist cannot create. It only means that he who has mastered the language will not have to worry about technical problems.

In a general sense, if the years you spend in learning can make you able to solve simple technical problems in your painting, then, because of them, you will have more than enough of a foundation to build your dreams on. For example, the advanced student would have this foundation if he can set up a still life of two or three simple objects, and then have the technical experience to paint the still life well, including the basic compositional skill to make the still life convey his vision and engage the viewer's curiosity and desire to want to keep looking at the still life painting. The student also needs enough knowledge of what quality means to avoid the look of amateurish work and some sort of wisdom to maintain a certain vision. If the student achieves just these basic elements, then he is set to go. The rest will come according to the challenges the student faces in the real world and how open he is to growth.

The same principles are true for painting portraits, landscapes, figures and compositions. Experience, a good sense of what quality is and vision are what a student has to leave a studio with.

Almost all students after some years of study will gain some reliable confidence and a method of technically solving problems, but in order to be secure and have this problem solving so ingrained that it becomes secondhand to him, the student has to work the same way for some time, two years or more. If students do not worry about what they don't know but do only what they can do best, they will without any doubt develop a technical skill that will be unique and suitable to their temperament. Of all the students I have had contact with, those who show up and keep doing what they remember is required of them without worrying about what they don't know learn faster and in time become good at some sort of technique that belongs solely to them.

Using Different Materials to Create Art

Because of the strong and unique personality built into artists' genetic makeup, or DNA, it is normal that they like to work in a way that suits their personal temperament. Because of this impulse and the freedom built into creativity to work "as one wishes," almost all artists work differently, even if they are using the same materials or have been influenced by the same teacher. This is why the student should not get too caught up in his likes and dislikes of style, taste and preference for materials before they have learned how to work with different kinds of materials. Rather students should just learn the use of basic materials and mediums, including tools such as paints, brushes, canvas, palette and palette knife.

As I've said repeatedly, it is not the materials that make the artist, but rather the message, the dream and the vision as well as the personal contribution. Depending on the artist's style or technique, he will use materials differently from other artists. The student need not worry about the different ways of using materials as long as he is enrolled in a professional environment. The student will learn how to use materials without even realizing it is happening. The versatility and broadness of knowledge of the instructor's teachings will be revealed in the works he shows in his portfolio or on the Internet. That's why the student should first investigate an instructor's work—and he should be sure see at least 15 to 20 works. Whether an artist's range is broad or not, it will come across in how he works. Fifteen works will tell more about an artist than a beautiful, professionally written résumé that lists a number of awards.

Whether you detest a particular medium or not, unless it is for health reasons, it is best to allow yourself to learn how to use and understand all the materials taught. These kinds of resentments of materials come about because the student is not logical and reasonable enough to remember why he enrolled in the class or to remember that he is paying to be taught. He is not aware that he is paying tuition to learn as much as he can about how art materials work. A new look and new usage can only make him more knowledgeable and broaden his scope. Students should be aware of the possibilities offered by mastering materials because not every instructor will have the patience to go out of his way to make efforts to convince the student that this is true or it is good for the student. Students with such close-minded attitudes have more to lose than their teachers.

For the sake of learning, it is always beneficial to adopt the practice of the learning environment that the student has decided to work in, rather than to pick and choose according to one's likes and dislikes.

John Singer Sargent and Claude Monet Painting Side by Side

There is a story about John Singer Sargent and Monet going out to paint together. During the painting session, Monet gave his palette to Sargent to try out. Sargent, who was from a very traditional background, was not used to a colorful palette without black. To Sargent, at that point, black was everything. Sargent looked at Monet and exclaimed, "How can I paint with a palette that has no black?" Monet, also an innovative colorist, holding Sargent's palette, looked at his friend and expressed a similar concern—he too held a palette without all the colors he was used to. How is it possible that one man's meat is another man's poison?

In Africa, during my early art education, I was taught first to draw a whole picture with a pencil, sometimes to trace, or pounce, the whole design, then to fill in with colors and paints. After my African art education, I went on to

Europe and there I learned the alla prima technique. At the Art Students League of New York, I met Oldrich Teply who taught me everything in the alla prima technique. My African training helped my imaginative skills and my European training helped me to understand realism. The combination gave me the freedom to work according to the subject or project. It is like being trained to be more accepting, and to turn on and off in any situation, to be spontaneous when necessary and cautious, studious and careful when it is required.

It would be very easy for me to list all my favorite materials and tell you how great or how useful they are. I could easily tell you what materials to chose and use. And I could swear by the list and give you all the logical reasons why they are the right materials. I could even give examples of the great masters who used the same materials and methods. But I would be very wrong to make such a point and to create the commandment that everyone should paint like me. It is useful to know that there are some experienced instructors out there doing some great stuff with their own choice of materials, most often using a very limited range of materials.

Materials differ from one artist to another. Materials do not make the art or the artist—the artist makes the materials. Therefore, the student's goal is only to learn how the materials work. It is the student's duty to be as flexible as possible in learning to use materials, never allowing himself to believe in one type of material or be brainwashed by the idea of "God's chosen material." Michelangelo did great things in fresco. Van Eyck created magical wonders with oil paints. Sargent achieved amazing dazzling effects with thick impasto while Ingres created some of the finest portraits with the thinnest layers of paint, using the glazing method.

Whoever the student studies with will determine what kind of the materials will be taught and the student should allow himself to learn, understand and use the assigned materials. Sargent was not so close-minded that he didn't try Monet's palette, nor was Monet too close-minded as to try Sargent's palette. If Van Gogh and Gauguin can stand near each other and paint together, then who has the Golden Secret to say what the Gods' chosen materials and methods are?

Almost every professional artist has his own set of materials that works well for him. As simple as it might sound, one artist might religiously like a certain set of materials yet another artist might hate those same materials passionately. Until the student graduates and finds materials that work well for him, he should be flexible with the materials his instructor suggests he use.

Figure 37 COMPOSING WITH VALUES AND COLOR, *Untitled, The art of picture making depends on the students understanding of the content in this picture. How to balance and compose with Values and Color.*

Figure 38

CHILDE HASSAM
(1859-1935)
The Red Mill, Cos Cob,
1896, oil on canvas,
Courtesy of Adelson
Galleries, New York

Students should refrain from letting their likes and dislikes prevent them from learning and understanding materials. Don't forget that the goal is to learn as much as there is to know about using materials. Then you can decide what works for you based on experience and knowledge. This attitude makes it easy and flexible for the student to adapt to the new environment without prejudices and resentment. The student will also learn more when he does not have reservations about taking in information.

As I have pointed out in the proceeding chapters, the greatness of artists mainly lies in their vision, ideas and contributions, never in the way they use materials and technique. Considering the tuition and time involved in mastering the techniques, the student should not put personal preferences before his education. The student's duty is to learn to know how, when and where to use any material being taught. After the student completes school he will then have the necessary knowledge to say yes or no to various materials.

CHAPTER ◄08◄

ARTISTIC STYLES AND VISION

Finding Your Unique Artistic Style

Note the technical differences between Van Gogh and Gauguin. These technical differences are what make their styles differ from each other so much. They are the alla prima and glazing techniques. Style develops from how pictures are painted and the materials used. Because of this it is inevitable that everyone who works at mastering the science of painting will, along the way, find his own personal style. Eventually, the student too will end up with his own style; therefore he should not spend too much time trying to find his style in the beginning. It is a waste of energy and time, trying to find yourself and your style. You are yourself.

New York City, because of the influx of teachers, has become like a buffet of art styles. If your appetite is big enough, you can order Rembrandt for breakfast, Leonardo for lunch and Picasso for dinner. If Michelangelo is a bit too rough and aggressive on your tongue you can tell the chef to serve you Ingres. You can keep Monet, Rubens, Matisse and Van Gogh for appetizers! As you wish. So many choices make it very difficult to choose the right teacher. This is the main reason why you should do some homework before enrolling in any class.

The average student gets confused and doesn't know what to do with these choices. Imagine going to Leonardo's studio in the morning, then to Michelangelo's for lunch. Their characters and their temperaments differ so much—each sees, thinks and responds as a unique individual. To learn from Michelangelo and understand why he works in a certain way is to accept everything that makes him different—from the way he draws to how he thinks. You as a student can only gain the full benefit of his work by accepting him. Not by selecting a certain part of him and rejecting some other parts. This can be possible after you become a professional and have learned the basics; even then the museum will be a better source to learn from. On the other hand, if the advanced student feels there is something he can learn from an instructor, then it is best to find ways to consult the instructor in a very honest manner and tell the instructor his needs and see what suggestions the instructor will give.

Avoid stylized techniques that are too personal. Stylized techniques are very seductive and it is very difficult to undo the damages they cause; it will cost you in the future. It is inherent in all artists to be whom they are and what all artists need is to be the master of the basic method of painting so that they too can go on and find their own approach.

As a student your talent and abilities deserve the teaching skill, knowledge, ideas and challenges that can bring the best out of you. A style in its natural form is just the special way each individual artist uses the material to solve problems in order to express or convey his messages. A style is the signature of an individual artist and suits that particular artist better than it would any other artist. Sometimes one artist will prefer to add more oil to his medium than to use thick paint. Painters like Ingres might not like any visible brushstrokes, while an artist like Sargent will prefer that the heavier pigment be part of his art. Monet will prefer to capture subtle nuances by using choppy strokes while Degas would rather unify and organize his work and paint from a foundational plan.

Naturally, our background, temperament and taste play some role in how we reach a certain personal style; the student will have to have confidence or trust that, without any effort on his part, without ever trying or searching too hard, he will someday find his own style no matter what.

Choosing instructors is not like going to a buffet bar to pick just what you want. The student has to choose intelligently and wisely; he has to choose with his head and mind—not too much with his heart. He will have to invest several years in his studies. Therefore, he should make smart decisions and careful choices about whom to study with. The choices he makes can prolong his education and affect what he learns, so he should choose a qualified professional artist and stick with him or her. He should commit to someone with a solid foundation and then see if they have all the alphabets, syllabus and grammar needed to teach him what he needs to learn. While he might not like one side of the teacher he can learn to accept or adopt the whole package. Trying every

Figure 39

A CLASS PROJECT, *Treating colors as Mosaic*

style and technique and not developing his personal sensitivity, not knowing anything well or not understanding and mastering one method, a student often leaves school with an incomplete way of handling artistic problems and some-times with incompatible skills.

Figure 40

SAMUEL ADOQUEI,
Eymet, France

It is not by coincidence that the average person who eats at the buffet bar is more overweight than the one who brings his or her own boring lunch or goes to a special eatery or restaurant. The same thing eventually happens to the art student. He who studies everywhere and does not commit to one place, who goes back and forth between teachers, will not be eating a healthy diet.

It is inevitable that all painters who follow a traditional way of learning will, one way or another, be influenced by their teacher at times. It is in the nature of the art field. Picasso was influenced by Cézanne, and Cézanne by Raphael. Every artist has been influenced by some other artist at one time or another and every artist will always be influenced by someone else; the honest artist will acknowledge this and embrace it. It is natural and students should embrace the idea. Emulating an artist you admire is a common and natural practice among all artists during the early stages of their education.

It is natural and it is best to embrace it rather than to fight against it, as long as the artist is emulating or imitating in order to learn. This is a way of using that artist's work as a sort of springboard or head start. Whether the stu-dent will go on to evolve his own style or not depends on the student. Because we all have different goals and aims as artists, we will follow different paths to finding our own personal destination. Some will reach their destination by air, some by land, others by bus, while some by foot. This process of artists reach-ing their own personal destination or achieving their personal goals is the way all great artists differ from each other despite who they were influenced by.

Sometimes, one can wonder why Zorn, Sorolla and Sargent used exactly the same style, yet their unique personal vision did not box them in or narrow them. Raphael and Leonardo also never got boxed in although they used similar techniques. In modern times the layman has been convinced that he must believe in the idea that being different is what art is all about. This has made every layman think he is an expert. This kind of thinking makes it impossible for the art student to concentrate on the right way of studying—the result is that a student is more likely to think they know what is good for them in art classes. Only the few lucky students who are well informed make the right decisions that lead them to succeed.

In some way, since all realistic, or representational, artists use the same grammar to portray their vision and ideas, it can appear on the surface as if they have a very limited vocabulary. However, the numbers used by accountants and mathematicians are only ten, but the sky is the limit as to what they can do with these ten numbers. In representational art, styles are among the easiest things to achieve. Yet true style actually comes to the artist when he is not trying to find it or thinking about it.

How Do You Find Your Own Style?

Despite all the basic grammatical laws for the construction of languages, the sound of each person's voice is uniquely his own; it has a natural accent which is made up of such things as tone and rhythm, that is, until he forces himself to speak like someone else. Otherwise, our unique and personal accent only changes with age and experience. Our painting style follows the same pattern. You are your style if you remain true to yourself; if you are honest and natural, you will just have to paint by responding to your likes and dislikes guided by the basic technical skills you have acquired. Thankfully, our beautiful uniqueness is embedded in our genetic make up. It is much easier to maintain our personal style than we think.

Because of our natural differences, we will always have different styles despite our training. We will gravitate to a certain unique way of solving problems and we will all respond to nature differently. A rigidly trained artist will still find himself attracted to certain subject matter and will explore particular aspects of nature. In color, some artists will explore the softer and more somber side of nature (the mauves), while others will explore the strong chromatic colors and blues or greens.

To find the style that suits your taste, pay attention to things that please you most and the things that inspire you to paint. Start exploring those things as you move into your advanced student period and, when out of school, make a conscious plan to explore your passions. Explore that which appeals to you with devotion, hard work and seriousness. Most artists with a sincere vision will not have to worry about what they paint because they will find themselves going back to a certain subject matter over and over again.

Without an intensive exploration of your preferred subject matter the results of what you create might come across as lacking in sensitivity and sincerity. Study the Old Masters and their differences and consider how well they explored the field and capitalized on their unique differences. No one else will be able to go along the same path that you will follow and explore it as you do. Our place in history depends upon how well we show the world how important and wonderful is our unique and rare vision.

Can You Change Your Existing Style?

The fact that you want to change your existing style means you have been working in a way that does not suit your temperament, suppressing your freedom and approaching your work in a way you might innocently have thought was the only way. You might have chosen that certain way without being aware of it.

The way to change old habits and find out what pleases your desires and temperament is:

a) The next time you start a painting, approach it with no set of do's and don'ts. Be true, honest and natural and respond to the subject with a practical and logical mind, that is where beauty of style is; there is no one way of working, no matter what you think. Ten true honest artists in a studio with the same subject will produce works that will look different. Only ten followers who deny themselves the freedom to explore their talent will produce works that look alike. On the other hand, if you are confused, then be happy with how you are painting now.

b) The faster and quicker way to change is to make a strong conscious acceptance of the things you are lacking and the things you want, and for the goodness and improvement of your progress search well for what you want. Find an artist with the technical approach that you like and respond well to, an approach that suits your temperament, and study with that artist. Just remember not to try learning the new style and at the same time painting as you always have. It is best just to put aside your old ways and enrapture yourself with the new way. Approach your newly discovered way with a clear and open mind. In the old way that you are used to think, it may sound possible, but things don't work that way. Put your past experiences aside.

c) Copying your favorite paintings at museums or from good reproductions is a good way to break away from what you are used to. Don't be shy about asking your instructors if you can copy their work during this stage of searching. But don't copy two opposing styles at the same time. It is too confusing. For example, don't copy Rembrandt and then Monet. If Rembrandt has what you think you want to learn, copy the styles that fall into Rembrandt's category. If not, then copy the work of other artists whose style you like.

Figure 41 SAM ADOQUEI, *Death of An American President*

Can You Create Your Own Style?

You are your genetic makeup. Can you change your DNA? You are how you observe and how you make decisions as to what to select from your observations. You are how you see nature and paint it; you are your style and technique whenever you are not following a set of restricted rules, so be honest, true and natural and your true self will proudly jump out of your subconscious and appear on your canvases. But try painting like someone else and you will find yourself feeling dishonest and "the true you" will give way to that programmed you.

Style is like an addictive drug, but more illusive and very dangerous, and it is the hardest thing to get rid of once you have adopted a certain unnatural style. Several paintings hanging on the same wall painted with the same style will lose a certain charm that the work of honest artists possesses. Skill confers most of the keys needed to open the gates of success for artists. The one thing a student who wants to keep his eye on the artistic priority list should concentrate on is skill before style.

Why Not Master the Basics in Order to Have Some Freedom in the Future

The art and craft of painting is like all other professions. There are as many styles as there are artists but the rules of grammar stay the same. As with language—whether you intend to write novels, nonfiction, plays or poems, the most important lesson one has to learn in the beginning is the grammar, the structure of the language. It does not matter if one already speaks the language; choosing a specialized field as a profession is a totally different thing. One has to first learn the alphabet, then master some of the vocabulary, then form short phrases and short sentences and paragraphs, and so on. Often, short stories are the foundation of complicated longer stories.

The craft of art is like a language. The student has to learn and know and understand how to make or construct pictures in order to have full command to be able to do as he wishes rather than settle for accidental results that happen through incompetence. A student can spend two, three or even ten years learning and still not be able to paint well because of not being able to focus on the important things—the basics—and do what is necessary to handle first things first. On the other hand, I have seen students spending a very short time studying, maybe a couple of years, and they have left school to become good painters just because they focused on the basics and went about the process accordingly.

Freedom in art means having command over your skills, to be able to do what you want and what you like and to have total control to do as you wish.

YOUR VISION AND IDEAS

An artist without a vision is like an individual without a goal or without a special purpose in life, and without a vision, the artist will be attracted to everything and will pursue anything. It is that important vision that we see with our mind's eye that encourages us to pursue art and gives us reasons to live life as an artist. Yet without a conscious effort at maintaining and focusing on that vision, an unimportant thing can sway the artist into being something else. And without technical skills to support the vision the artist can be misunderstood and without personal artistic style the artist will get lost among other artists. For the artist, a personal vision is the most important part of keeping his uniqueness.

From the past to the present, it is the quality of the artist's vision that separates one artist from another. Technical skills clarify an artist's vision and make it stand out and easy to understand. Vision is what art enthusiasts admire; it is the quality scholars respect in artists. Even though it requires skill to express a message so that it hits its intended target, for an artist to show that he has a vision does not necessarily require a whole lot of skill. But it requires skill to make the vision easy to understand. No matter how great and grand a vision is, if not assisted by a good technique, the work will not express its intended message. Style when taken literally can come across like vision, yet style and vision are miles apart.

Style is the way the artist personally uses his materials, giving the artwork a certain kind of look. An artist can therefore imitate a style in order to support his vision. It is like this for all creative artists, writers and musicians, even leaders and political leaders, etc. The main reason for some artists' fifteen minutes of fame is the overly ambitious dreams and visions that those artists have, artists who don't have enough skill to support these visions. The solidness of an artist's reputation depends on technical skills, style and vision. And it will be these qualities that the artist can build his reputation on. As the public becomes more and more educated, the public will start differentiating—expecting these qualities from artists.

Everyone can have big dreams and big visions, but the artist has to pay his dues by acquiring skills in order to communicate well with the public.

In recent years, it has become common to have technique and style but no

Figure 42 SAM ADOQUEI, *Dee in Prayers, oil on canvas*

vision, or to have vision but no technique. An artist can also have technique and vision but no style. Of these three essential qualities that serve as the backbone of any good artist. Style is the only element an artist can do without but luckily it is the only element that comes without too much effort. On the other hand it is not advisable to ignore the cultivating of technique and vision. Technique and vision, when cultivated and improved upon, make the pursuit of art very easy and enjoyable. These two alone can hold onto an artist's reputation. It is easy to achieve greatness at one time but to maintain the greatness for ages takes a timeless, universal vision.

Vision to the artist literally means the artist's unique way of seeing the world, the choices and selections he makes after observing the world around him—what the artist imagines and sees with his mind's eye and brings out by way of his art. Vision is also what the artist's unique imagining conscience tells him about how the world ought to be. The more noble the artist's subconscious mind is the more likely the artist's vision will also be noble. Even though the artist is capable of doing the opposite of what his subconscious mind tells him to do, for the most part, artists are influenced by their subconscious mind, which means that what the artist creates is what his vision is and what his conscious and subconscious mind are.

On the surface it might look as if vision is the hardest thing to have for artists. Yet it is the only part of the artistic talent that comes automatically with an artist's DNA. It can develop or change with age and life experiences, yet sometimes it remains the same. Circumstances and conditions can influence the artist visions and ideas. For example, an artist can be sympathetic towards a war, and his visions of the war can remain the same and can stay that way for years. He may portray images that promote peace, while another artist's vision depicts beauty by painting flowers and other naturally beautiful things. But his can change with experience, and the same artist will end up portraying other things. Life experience have more influence on how an artist's vision changes than biological or gender factors.

For the artist to have a unique vision, he must be as honest as possible. In the arts, it is not as bad to copy an artist's style as it is to copy his vision. Vision is unique to one artist; it is built up totally through all that makes that artist into who he is: his beliefs, experiences, ideas, his ups-and-downs, his temperament, taste, wishes and philosophical thinking. So, to copy another artist's vision is to almost change your name and take on that artist's name.

In order for the artist to develop his vision, he should live a life of constantly drawing his inspirations for his creations from nature, creating without too many preconceived notions; he should respond to his inner feelings and observe the part of nature that he finds untapped. There are still hidden treasures in nature, awaiting the honest and curious artist. He should select from the natural world the only things he personally thinks are worthy of the images in his mind's eye, images that he strongly believes can represent what his contributions and legacies to society are. He should be very personal in all his creative decisions. He should avoid being influenced in his subject matter by other artists. He should be strong enough to withstand criticism. He should be honest and very sincere in his selection of subjects, sincere and honest enough that anything apart from what his heart desires will not be worthy enough for the purpose of living the artistic life. It is this noble idea of contribution to society that makes life worthy of living for the artist and makes art the right medium to convey this purpose.

The artist's specialty is that through what he sees and believes he can directly or indirectly contribute to mankind's life. The artist should do whatever feels sincere and natural within reason. One cannot be that wrong when ideas come out of broad knowledge. The experienced artist should cut off all the programmed ideas he has inherited, and only do what comes natural to him. Instead of worrying about what to create, he should just create. The artist should just do anything he feels comfortable doing with a thoughtful attitude. Even if what he envisions comes across as odd, he should always remember that odd things are part of man's being and the artist has to explore that odd vision in order for it to have meaning. If the ideas behind the odd vision make us look at life differently or make us reason differently, then it's a good vision. And by finding answers to these questions, we may stumble on ideas that will help improve society. That then is a good answer.

Besides commercialization, publicity and advertising, vision is the part of the artist's achievement or legacy that helps his reputation endure for the ages. Because culture changes, times change, men change and priorities change; almost all of men's experiences change. Whether a vision will endure or change with the times depends on how grand, how universal, how timeless the vision is. This is more obvious in politics than in the arts. The political figure whose vision is to help all men will have a more enduring vision than the politician who just wants to get reelected.

The same goes for musicians. The musician whose aim is to compose works in order to provide hope for everyone can do so only if he proceeds along a sincere and noble course in life. A writer might have a vision but he will still have to use the English language in reality. It is not all the time that one's vision is embraced and accepted. Sometimes, it is not embraced until the artist is long gone. It is for this reason that most experienced artists develop several skills. Ideally, it is for this reason that all students should learn to be versatile; develop the skills and temperaments to produce commercial works as well as the temperament to make creative works (your vision) and the temperament to experiment with innovation. Any artist with this versatility is likely to succeed in any civilized culture.

The beginning student shouldn't worry too much about vision and style, because they are part of the artistic being; they are so embedded in the artist's being that it would take a lot of effort to lose them; most experienced artists pick them up along the way. That's why in the chapter on the stages of the artist, I did not make them part of the priority list. Skill, technique, experience and knowledge are on top of the list and style and vision come afterwards. Style and vision are what the advanced student should pay attention to once he is out of school; then traits such as style and vision might appear. In order to have a clear and enduring vision the artist will need to depend on his technical skills, to vividly clarify his vision so that he stands out from other artists. And for that, the artist will have to rely on a very unique style. A style that cannot be missed when the work is seen among that of other artists.

Working from Photographs

In the beginning of your learning, avoid copying or practicing from photographs. This way of learning is not challenging enough for an ambitious student, and it will hinder your later progress and sometimes it might corrupt you forever. Of course, photography is always better than nothing. It is okay to use photographs if you don't have any other source of learning. But if you think you really want to pursue art seriously as a vocation, you will find that most professional teachers love to teach the basics.

Often students are reluctant to start off the right way, so the professor find himself helping students by letting them do what they want. However, using the camera is very addictive, once you start with the camera it is difficult to work from life. You can always use the camera after you've acquired skill and confidence in the technical area. When you develop your skill by depending on the camera, you are indirectly suppressing your artistic identity and corrupting your visual senses. The visual sense should be allowed to select and choose according to what the mind wants—that is all part of the training. The way you personally observe nature, respond to nature and portray nature are all part of the search for oneself.

All good instructors are aware of the limitations of working from photos in the beginning stages of a student's experience and they will not recommend using them even if they have to lose a student. As I said in the beginning, artists teach for different reasons, so giving the students what they want as a way of keeping them may be an individual instructor's choice. Always be happy when you find a teacher who works you hard at mastering the basics.

I don't advocate going to school and paying high tuition for years to learn to paint from photos—unless you are over 65 or 70, retired, ill or art is a hobby or a therapy. There is nothing wrong with professional artists using photography as a tool. I have seen many professionals taking advantage of the camera and doing beautiful work. I am sure that all successful professionals using photography were good painters long before they started using the camera. Consider that painting technique is not as hard as one might think—it can take a shorter time to learn the important basics than one imagines. Therefore, it is not worth the trouble of learning first from photography or copying from photographs.

To the beginning student, it might seem okay and fun to work from photographs, but one gets addicted to it. The student will find it very difficult to develop other important parts of his creativity and he may become impatient with the step-by-step process of learning the basics of painting. On the other hand, if the student has to be self-taught, then it doesn't matter as much what the student paints from. But even then I recommend the student start by copying from good prints of paintings by the Old Masters or paintings by contemporary painters the student likes.

Once the student decides to study art and give himself some years to go through his studies, then he, for his own benefit, should try as hard as he can not to paint with the assistance of the camera. During these years, he should mentally block out the camera as a tool, except when he is doing special projects for special purposes.

"Let everything be allowed to do what it naturally does,
so that its nature will be satisfied."
-Chuang Tzu

Figure 43

JOAQUIN BATISDA
y SOROLLA

*For posters of
Joaquin Sorolla's
work, call
(212) 926-2234
or visit www.
hispanicsociety.org*

CHAPTER ◂O9◂

THE IMPORTANCE OF DRAWING

"Draw, draw, draw. Draw, Antonio, draw." —Michelangelo's advice to his students
"Draw lines and draw lines." —Ingres' advice to Degas

From fine art drawing and painting to fashion design, cartooning, illustration and graphic design—in all the fields of art, there is no more valuable, important and useful thing to learn than how to draw. The art and science of painting consists of drawing and painting, yet in the beginning students tend to think the two are different and separate. While the artist who draws accurately might not be able to paint well, the painter who paints accurately draws accurately too because it takes drawing ability to paint accurately. Ideally, painting is a way of drawing with the brush.

Drawing is one of the skills that when learnt well can develop several parts of the student's artistic sensibilities: his concentration, carefulness, aggressiveness, patience, meditation, calmness and analytical senses. Just learning to do a certain exercise in drawing can develop all these. An exercise such as spending four weeks drawing a model in a single pose can develop the student's sense of calmness, while another exercise, doing one- to five-minute poses, can develop the artist's sense of aggression, making him think and work fast without mistakes; that is, to move fast while still paying attention to accuracy. One special type of drawing exercise can develop the student's meditative senses while another will improve on his ability to do two things at the same time.

If the student is lucky enough to enroll in an environment that has a complete curriculum, he will learn all these things without realizing it; that's why it is so important to be careful where you enroll and to consider what the students are being taught. All well-grounded professional artists have these skills and will teach them. These skills are often embedded in the materials and methods

Figure 44

DEAN CORNWELL,
Untitled

*A great painter and
illustrator, a draghts-
man whose work
should be studied by
students interested in
composing and put-
ting multiple figures
together.*

and chances are instructors only teach what is important and what suits a particular individual at a certain time, not what the student personally prefers or
feels good doing. Example: A student who does not understand all the exercises
and the kind of senses they are meant to develop might want to skip an exercise
because it is too fast or too slow for his taste.

The most valuable lesson is to develop the joy of drawing, to learn to develop your natural abilities without using devices—your EYE, MIND and HAND coordination.

The easiest, fastest and most efficient way of learning to draw and paint is by first drawing and painting simple objects. Before taking art classes, the student should develop the joy of drawing by copying from any reference material, such as photos and Old Master drawings. This helps self-taught students learn the basic natural methods; of developing their simple natural abilities of EYE, MIND and HAND coordination. without using devices.

It is also advisable not to attempt the life model and anatomy during your early stages as a student. It is hard to comprehend anatomy if the student has not developed basic drawing skills. Simple still life objects are the ideal subjects to learn to understand the basics of drawing. Even Leonardo da Vinci learned anatomy only after he knew enough about drawing and was ready to explore and specialize in the figurative arts. Only when a student has mastered the basics of how to look, how to judge proportions by measuring back and forth between the model and the paper and has, therefore, become advanced, will basic artistic anatomy be necessary.

Because of the differences in teaching styles and teaching methods, all teachers have different books that they suggest to students for their teaching curriculum. It is therefore much wiser to only use books recommended by your teacher. Such special books will be helpful to you during your course of study since it will be much easier to follow up the lessons by discussing the book with the one who recommended it. There are many books on drawing, but not all of them will be the right choice because not all drawing ideas are believed in by all instructors. Some books may be incompatible with your teacher's style or teaching methods.

Continually practice methodical traditional exercises—there are no shortcuts to drawing well. It is a waste of students' time and tuition to try and study from several different instructors with different approaches. I always suggest that students use a book or two; they should learn everything they can from one book before moving on to another.

The way an artist draws and uses color or composes and paints can tell you what is in their whole teaching package. A student only needs a mastery of the basics to be able to go out and build his own style and to pursue his vision. Getting the best of three to five instructors does not mean the student will come out with untouchable superman skills. Studying with many teachers rather backfires. Skill is learned by the continuous use of time-proven methods and through the development of time-proven habits that have worked for every artist in the past. If there are reasons beyond your control, such as travel or financial difficulties, that force you to change instructors, then that is a different issue. The consequences of playing clever by trying to outsmart yourself or the experienced instructor are not worth the cost.

At school a good program will first start you off drawing still life as well as plaster casts of simple objects like spheres, cubes, cylinders and objects with concave and convex surfaces. You will learn to create the illusion of space, light, atmosphere and mood. Practicing such simple exercises makes it easier for the beginner to comprehend how to draw and then to use that knowledge for more complicated and complex projects, such as portraits or figures with complex backgrounds as well as landscapes and interiors.

Drawing is the easiest skill to work with; everyone drew freely before they attended art school and almost any 9- to 15-year-old can draw well. It does not take any extra talent to draw well. At art schools, almost every student who wishes to draw well has always learned to draw well. The challenges that the student faces are in the teaching methods. Most good drawing teachers know what it takes so almost any good drawing teacher has the patience and a formulated method that helps students. Students, if patient and without unrealistic expectations, always end up learning to draw well. Once the basic methodical approach is understood, all the student needs to do is to have the patience to keep repeating the process until he masters it.

The more the student understands the field of art, the more he will realize how everything revolves around drawing; there is nothing a student cannot learn if he can draw well. Drawing techniques are applicable to all other techniques. The drawing approach applies observing, measuring and analyzing to solving the technical problems of art. It is the materials that change, not the techniques. From drawing, the student learns how to analyze, how to carefully respond to the sensitive sides of nature; the student learns tones, texture, edges and how line works; he learns values and many, many important things that he will need in the field of painting as well as in fashion design and graphic arts. Drawing is the most economical way to learn.

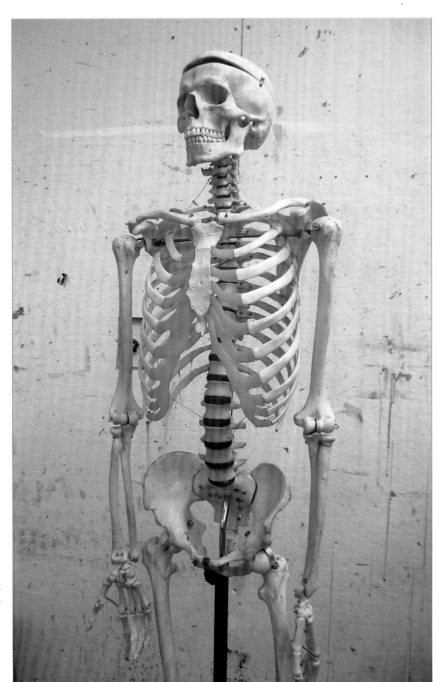

Figure 45

SKELETON,
Human anatomy is too complex to comprehend by beginners, before studying anatomy it is best for the student to develop some basic skills in drawing.

The Constructional Method of Drawing

There is a very simple and reliable method of drawing; it is a method that all drawing methods and styles are derived from. The constructional approach to drawing is the most time-proven method. When understood, this method of drawing allows the student to find his own path.

This method can be broken down thus: simplify everything into geometric, abstract shapes. In the early stages of drawing, this method is used to achieve accurate proportions. That is followed by the study of planes, forms and the direction of light sources. Then the student learns how to see complex details within the abstract shapes; eventually he will be able to sensitively render minute details.

Figure 46

A Hand by a student. (From the authors Union Square, New York, Atelier)

This process has to be repeated over and over again until using it becomes a second language to the art student. With this method fully understood and mastered, the student can explore and take chances with confidence without losing his way. This is a basic and general approach to drawing. The most important thing the student should be cautious about is to avoid learning stylized forms of drawing.

The Constructional Method Broken Down into Stages

First stage The student learns to see by determining the simple basic abstract shapes that make up the subject, such as a group of apples, then he uses angles to block-in the entire subject, either the full group of apples or he may crop part of the subject, so that his drawing includes only part of the group. The student proceeds without worrying about details, considering only the abstract shapes he sees. He divides the subject into a few bold abstract shapes. He makes sure to spend most of his time judging and worrying about the basic proportions, moving up and down the page, constantly checking how the right side relates to the left side and also how the upper part of the drawing relates to the lower part of the drawing. He checks how the parts of the drawing relate to each other vertically, horizontally and diagonally, from one corner to the other, finding points of reference and checking to see how the angles he is drawing line up with those points.

Making sure that they line up is the most important tool he uses to achieve correct basic proportions. He learns how the basic proportions relate to each other by constantly comparing and relating the simple abstract shapes to each other. The goal at this stage, as well as other stages, is to reduce nature to abstract shapes; the reason for doing this is that it is easy for the beginner to achieve good proportions when he is not too concerned with details.

Second stage Once the student has learned how to draw abstract shapes so that they represent natural objects, he moves on to massing or grouping the smaller parts that the subject is made up of in order to learn how the parts of the subject relate to each other. He does not learn "ideal" proportions but learns to draw proportions based on the subject he is working on. Whether the student can achieve good proportions or not depends on how well and how constantly he compares and relates the masses to each other. The student now begins to pay attention to the planes of the three-dimensional parts within the subject. He also learns how to work the shapes of light and shade against each other, through which the direction of the light source will be indicated. The student will have to make considerable effort to be aware of the direction of the light source; his success also depends on how habitually the student remembers to repeat the process.

Third stage The student now moves on to details within the masses, sensitively working on clarifying planes and studying the direction of the light source. At this stage a lot of attention is spent on understanding the planes and the light—a quick tonal study will be used to suggest light and shade. The student will work on playing the shapes of light against the shapes of the darks, achieving a very sculptural and graphic effect. From here on, the student can do more work on clarifying details of parts of the subject, never forgetting to constantly compare and relate angles. The student will also work on slow, minutely rendered studies of form with gradually added shading. The main goal at the third stage is for the student to increase his sensitivity towards nature and to pay attention to nature-hidden information.

Fourth stage The student learns to pay attention to details in order to learn and understand more about how subjects differ as well as to reveal something new about the subjects, that which can be revealed only through intensive study. It is this approach that develops the student's sensitivity and uniqueness. And it is this uniqueness that when developed properly brings out the artist's vision.

The technical method I have just explained has nothing to do with materials, style or a particular tradition. It forms a general, logical and formal technical approach to drawing. Through using this method, you will achieve good proportions in your drawings and good drawing skills. This method is used to transform three-dimensional objects into accurate proportional drawings on a two-dimensional surface.

This methodical drawing process can be broken down into five stages that the student should work hard to understand and master while in school:

How to construct with angles in the beginning stages of a drawing.

How to use simple abstract shapes to generalize complicated and complex real things so that good proportions can be achieved by looking at and comparing the simplified shapes.

How to understand and render the planes of three-dimensional objects and how to draw light by understanding how it falls on an object. How shapes of light and shade play against each other in life. How to understand the transitions between forms and how to zoom in to tackle minute details in order to capture character.

How to train the visual analytical senses: looking, comparing, analyzing while making sure that good proportions are achieved.

How to do quick sketches of 1, 5, 10 and15 minutes in order to be able to draw the figure in a more realistic setting than in a studio where all the models are

Figure 47

JOHANN CHRIS-
TIAN REINHART,
German (1761-1847)
Goat

professionals. It is important to fill several sketchpads with this exercise and then have an experienced person go over the proportions with you. Besides what is covered in stage 3 above, this is the most valuable skill I learned in drawing. How to focus or zoom in on details in order for the student to develop a patient sensitivity towards nature.

Other forms and styles of drawing that train different senses, such as contour drawing and gesture drawing, are good for a student who has some prior understanding of the basic general approach to drawing. All experienced artists eventually find ways they like to draw and discover what they feel comfortable doing, but for students, the basic understanding of the drawing process and what to do from start to finish is needed so that they can go on to find their own style of drawing.

Basic Drawing
There is no myth to drawing.

Unless you are very advanced and can draw very well, always draw in whatever painting class you have enrolled in. This is the best way to be introduced to how painters think, work and solve problems. Drawing is not only about learning anatomy, proportions and style, or even shading techniques—drawing is also about developing the different senses of the artistic mind; it is about how an artist thinks about his subject, what he selects, what he investigates, what he explores, and what he leaves out.

The only way to know why an artist does things a certain way is to understand why and how they like to draw. Therefore, if you want to learn under someone, it pays to learn about that artist's whole experience: How they draw, why they draw and what they draw. By going through this process of how and why and what, the student will then have a better understanding of that artist's work. If you draw like Van Gogh, you will paint like Van Gogh. If you draw with the sensitivity of Picasso, you will paint like Picasso. You can't draw like Picasso, think like Van Gogh and paint like Sargent; it might seem possible, but it is not. So, no matter how good a student is, it is more helpful to always draw with the artist he is studying or learning under. Unless, the artist (the teacher) suggests other exercises, it is always a clever idea to do a certain exercise recommonded by the teacher. Drawing exercises are designed by the teacher to make the student learn different aspects of the teacher's teaching procedure and also to learn about nature, in addition to just getting accurate proportions and rendering what he sees. Besides this, learning construction in order to achieve basic proportion is the ideal priority for a beginner. There is no myth to drawing. Everyone can learn to draw well.

YOUR SPECIAL DRAWING SENSES

Learning Eye, Mind and Hand Coordination

To understand nature the student must draw with all his senses.
The mind, before making judgments, should consult the eyes, and the hand should learn to obey what the eyes have seen and the mind has questioned.

   The beginner has to learn basics; only then can he proceed to learning how to understand complex things like form, value, color, drawing and composition. When learning to draw, the student's goal should be to learn to construct, understand, dissect, or research the subject they draw. Drawing should train the student's analytical senses. The purpose of drawing is not just to copy or to

Figure 48 SAM ADOQUEI, *Copy after Rembrandt, Durer, Ribera and birds and friends.(etching).*

PETRVS BREVGEL
ANTVERPIÆ PICTOR RVRALIVM ACTIONVM.

Figure 49 ANTHONY VAN DYKE, *Portrait of Pieter Bruegel*

achieve a realistic rendition of the subject or to display pencil skills. Because of these goals of how the drawing looks on the surface rather than what the student learns from the subject, several students I have known can show portfolios of impressive drawings, yet when faced with a life model they find it difficult to produce similar impressive results.

Many drawings now have more shading than the drawings of the Old Masters of the Renaissance period. When the student studies drawings by the Old Masters, he will notice that the drawings were done for the purpose of learning from the experience and developing analytical sensitivities, sensitivities towards nature, rather than just copying or drawing as a platform for the exhibition of fancy shading techniques. The student nowadays, if not careful, can be sucked into these competitions of fancy shading skills and they will forget about the real reasons and purposes for learning to draw. Drawing is a way to understand and to achieve good proportions, correct planes and textures as well as to help the artist learn to work from memory. These are also the reasons why the student should make every effort to read as much as he can about the subject. The student should continuously do research in order to see examples of the drawings of the great Old Masters and also to gather similar ideas and to learn the reasons why some techniques might be more important than others at certain times of the student's learning period. If he does not, he is in danger of being attracted to gimmicks not helpful to his growth.

If, on the other hand, the reader is not a student but a professional artist, and prefers to create his art by displaying shading techniques and skills, then may the angels and saints of shading give him abundant knowledge in those areas and help him achieve beautiful tonal qualities. And, if that's the case, then the reader should be aware of the purpose of this book. The professional can use the book as a reference. But this book is for students who want to do the right thing before pursuing the study of art, hoping to gather some knowledge or ideas about the field in order to plan well before starting.

Stories from the Studio
"Where the spirit does not work with the hand there is no art."
—Leonardo da Vinci

The Blind Portrait Artist
A friend of mine mentioned to me the birthday wishes of his 11-year-old daughter, who was half blind. He said she wanted portrait-drawing lessons as her 12th birthday gift from me. After several attempts to discourage the girl had failed he decided to mention it to me to see if I could come up with realistic reasons why she, being half blind, should not consider drawing from life. I wanted to take on the challenge of teaching a half-blind young artist, so I spent almost three months preparing exercises to teach the girl.

A day before her birthday, it dawned on me how impossible the task was. How can a blind girl enjoy drawing from life when some artists with perfect eyesight cannot do life drawing after years of training? It also dawned on me which senses a good artist draws with. The good sincere artist draws with all his senses: mind, eyes, knowledge and heart. Greatness depends on knowing which of these senses you have most developed and taking it to the extreme— taking fullest advantage of that sense that you feel secure in. An artist would rather be very good and knowledgeable at one thing than mediocre at everything. Hours before the birthday, I thought about the senses that this blind girl might have, and then formulated a way to go in and let her work on that.

She was very happy to hear me walk in, but a bit disappointed knowing that I didn't bring any materials or books to work with. She had a sketchpad and all the necessary drawing materials ready for me, and then she asked me, "Is it a lame idea, Mr. Adoquei, for me to want to draw portraits from life?"

"No, not at all," I replied. "I have come because I think it is a brilliant idea. You will enjoy drawing from life more than some artists who can see, but don't try to see."
"Oh really?" she replied.
"Yes, I am sure of it," I answered.
"Mary, you know every one of us has something so unique, so special and sometimes we have an abundance of it, but we don't use it enough or take advantage of it. Let's start whenever you are ready."
"I am ready, what should I draw with? Pencil or charcoal?"
"Who would you want to draw? I asked.
"I want to draw my father's friend, Mr. Son Mehaja. He is a doctor and he is a very nice man. He always tells me stories about Indian symbols, and I like him a lot."
"Where is he from?" I asked.
"He is from Bombay, India," she answered.
"How old is he?" I asked.
"I don't know," she said, "but I can ask my dad."
"What does he like to eat when he visits your father?"
"Some days he likes vegetables; I think he likes to drink lots of tea."
"Okay, let's start our classes. First, I want you to think of Larkmir, a 47-year-old doctor from India and from Bombay. He is a kind man and likes people; he also likes vegetables and he likes the color bluish-grey. Combine these descriptions of your father's friend and see this picture of him with your mind's eye. Make a mental picture, so that you can see him as a drawing on your wall. I want you to look at that picture you see with your mind's eye for ten minutes. Record it in your memory, and then copy what you see in your mind's eye for only three minutes. After that, look again at that picture you see with your mind's eye for ten minutes, and then draw for only three minutes. Repeat the process until you finish or you need me, then call me."

After forty-five minutes, I called to Mary. "Do you need me?
"No," she said, "I am trying to capture his lips. What do you think Sam?"
"You know, Mary, there was a great musician who wrote wonderful emotional music that moved and touched millions of people of all times from everywhere. He was deaf. He knew he could not hear but he could feel and imagine so he used his sense of feelings to imagine what the written music would sound like and what that sound should do. He wrote music according to how he felt and imagined. His name was Ludwig van Beethoven."

The reason why some art has more feeling than other art is because the good artist draws with other senses besides his technical abilities. Try responding to your subject. (Read also Angel Gabriel.)

I have a student in one of my classes who is working on her drawing technique. Her drawing always expresses the most delicate sensitive feelings. I am always amazed how, without much technical experience, she still manages to pull off these beautiful sensitive drawings that are more effective than some advanced drawings. When I was proofreading this book I thought of her, then I realized that she is always sympathetic towards the models, she always talks to them and often tells me how the models like a pose. She even knows the models' previous careers, their stories and their worries. To her, the models are humans who are posing rather than just entities for the students to draw.

The early stages of learning to draw are about developing the analytical senses. Eventually, the student must learn to develop his sensitivities and his mind, so that a face is not just a face, but also a unique individual from a special background with special experience. The last skill to learn in drawing is the creative approach—how to create, imagine and memorize an image.

With these abilities in drawing, there is nothing the student can't do. In reality, any student with these abilities alone can pursue almost any branch of the arts. Even though technically an artist can capture a character using these scientific skills, I like to emphasize that in fact the student should always be sensitive and observant. The artist can achieve so much with just honest observation of the subject at hand.

Drawing Materials

Simple materials are good enough.
A pencil and paper are all you need in the beginning.

There are a number of materials that are used for drawing; the most common ones are **pencil, charcoal, pastel, conté crayon** and **silverpoint.** One can
draw with anything that will make a mark. Sometimes the student will even
have to draw with the brush, using paint diluted with turpentine and linseed oil.
Charcoal and pencil are more traditional mediums and most instructors will
want students to start with one or the other. Other materials could be used, but I
recommend charcoal or pencil. They are more effective for the student.

Charcoal is more tonal and can be painterly, yet is precise enough to indi-

Figure 50 JAN MANKES, *Young Goat near Lake*

cate details; it helps the student make an easy transition to drawing with the brush. Charcoal is very versatile and has unlimited qualities. It is a good prelude to the grisaille method of dealing with tones and values in painting and it also makes it easy for students to use pastels if they decide to. The transition from charcoal to painting is easier to comprehend for beginners than the transition from lead pencil to painting.

Pencil is also very useful for several important reasons. Pencil, because of its sharp point (or preciseness) can help the student learn to achieve details. By using pencil the student develops the sensitivity to render detailed information. Pencil helps students focus on details in small sections of a subject. By using pencil the student learns to focus. (Always ask your instructor for suggestions.) The beginner might have some preferences, but it is more important to just learn to use whatever the teacher suggests. Even though it can be used in a manner similar to charcoal, it is wise to use pencil in the manner natural to it.

The student should first concentrate on the method of drawing, because it is the method that helps the student learn what is important, the methodical approach to achieving accurate proportions. If the student can spend the time it takes to learn to understand and achieve accuracy in basic proportions, nothing else is all that important, Achieving basic proportions requires repeating the drawing method over and over, continuously practicing with advanced assistance. Someone more experienced than the student is needed to check and double-check as well as correct the student's work. One of the main reasons why simple pencil or charcoal will do for learning is that in learning to draw the student's main concern is how he develops his faculty of observation. He needs to learn how to relate the objects he sees to each other, how to measure the distances between the objects and how to compare the parts of what he sees to each other. What the materials produce is not as relevant as what the mind learns. The student keeps repeating the same method until the approach becomes a second language. He can always learn to understand or play with other materials after he has learned the principles of drawing.

Figure 51 DEAN CORNWELL, *Untitled*

CHAPTER ◂O1O▸

DIFFERENT PAINTING METHODS

The only myth in painting is not finding or accepting the logical and scientific method to solve technical problems; it is as easy as drawing.

The technique and methods of painting still life, portrait, figure and landscape are all the same but the freedom or the constraints of the subject make each feel or look different. The way various types of drawing materials develop different aspects of our senses, so too can the kind of subject the student paints develop a certain part of the student's painting skills—figures and portraits, for example, often go through several stages of assessment and in this comparing back and forth, the student learns to pay careful attention. For the figure or portrait to be correct, the student has to use every little cell in his analytical senses. Years of this sensitive attention develops the student's analytical sensitivities.

In the approach to painting the figure falls in between the three types of painting methods I explained in the previous chapters. The first is drawing the composition first with pencil or charcoal and then filling it in with paint. The second is doing a tonal grisaille study before painting. The third way is working directly without any previous planning—the painter starts and hopes to finish in one sitting. This is known as the alla prima method. Some of my professional friends work in the first method I gave—the figure is drawn first in pencil and then gradually painted. I personally prefer to use the grisaille method, the second method. For me, there is more freedom in working this way. But I do the drawing for my mural paintings in pencil or charcoal before starting the actual painting.

Still life is the most practical subject to start with in learning to paint or

draw; it is also the most logical and beneficial. Every student who starts art school should try to avoid the student's desire to start with the figure instead of starting with something more simple and basic—even if the student hasn't had any previous training in still life painting. So many precise elements have to be aligned in figure and portrait painting in order for the end result to look decent that it is often frustrating and discouraging for the beginner to go straight to the figure. Still life painting does not have the constraints of figure painting. For that matter, it is just easier for the beginner to learn quickly the techniques of oil painting by painting still life and it is less stressful. In most good environments, the instructor will know what is best for the student. Often instructors suggest things because of their own preferences, so it is best, if you

Figure 52
(above)

SAM ADOQUEI,
Repose, oil on canvas

Figure 53
(above right)

SAMUEL ADOQUEI
Catfish

trust your instructor, to follow his suggestions. When in doubt, do what your instructor suggests; most instructors will know what is best for you.

No matter what the situation, the student should not learn to paint landscapes from photographs. More than working in any other subject, working from real landscape increases the student's ability to generalize complicated details. The nature of landscape lends itself to how it should be painted. Figure, still life and portrait all have some sort of inherent, logical method that even the inexperienced student can start with, and with time, get somewhere. This is not the case with landscape. Looking at a landscape, it would seem that it could be painted just using your common sense, but landscape is actually not that easy. Until you watch someone painting a landscape, it is very difficult to start on your own and figure out how it should be handled. Of course if you keep on going out to the field and struggling long enough the saints of landscape painting might reveal some problem-solving secrets to you.

For this reason the advanced student, or even any other artist who wants to try his hand at painting landscape, will save himself much time and frustration by taking a summer workshop in landscape painting. No matter how clever or advanced the student or the artist is some points he will learn in a summer class will save him several years of frustration and blaming of the saints. In the summer class, a very good landscape teacher will simplify the process and make a complex landscape easy to paint or draw. Most landscape workshops are conducted in the summer, and considering the summer is only three months of the year, there are many months in between workshops for the new painter of landscape to practice and to master the necessary principles.

If the artist is a bit shy about taking a workshop, just remember history is full of accomplished painters learning new ways of solving problems from their peers. A sincere friend who thinks he is helping a friend can open up lots of things. Workshops are the way to learn things the advanced student may otherwise never get the opportunity to learn.

ANATOMY OF A PAINTING

For any good painting to successfully communicate its message to the target, the painting's components (the elements used in constructing the painting) have to work in harmony. The artist has to understand how these elements work. Every now and then the artist might accidentally create a successful artwork, but in order to keep repeating the same success, the artist needs to know what constitutes a successful artwork, which components make up the anatomy of a painting. The anatomy of a painting consists of subject, materials, technique, style, composition and skill. A good painting by a professional artist is not created by accident or by talent alone but by knowing how the elements and components work, and using these elements to their full advantage.

Whether a painting holds together and delivers its message or not depends on how orderly, calculated and strategic the elements in the painting are put together. The components and their elements have do's and don'ts, and they should be learned well and understood well. This is something the art student should understand and master while at school. A creative work can be achieved or can come into being by accident but in most cases artworks are first conceived in the subconscious. Then the conscious mind formulates the idea and figures out how it can become a reality (using materials and technique). This is where knowledge and experience become necessary. The artist then plans and puts the subject matter together through gathering of the props that make up the subject and the materials to be used in executing the artwork. He composes the subject by arranging and rearranging the components (in the form of colors, values, lines, shapes, textures, etc.). Even if the results came about through accident, the accidental results are kept as final results, because only an experienced artist can recognize a good accident and the good qualities that are working beneath the accidental results.

The artist decides what style and what technique best suit the subject so

Figure 54

SAM ADOQUEI,
*Untitled (Study of
Flesh Tones with
Painting Knife)*

*Of all the painting
materials, palette
knife is the most
effective. when devel-
oping color mixing
abilities. The knife
forces you to make
definite mixing deci-
sions, by repeatedly
using the knife, the
artist's color mixing
skills develop.*

that the right effect that best communicates the right message is achieved by
using the available skills that the artist has acquired through his education and
working experience. Learning the how and why of paintings becomes the main
concern of a student during his years of studies. Even though it might seem that
there is too much to learn, the student need not worry because it is only the

Figure 55
(left)

SAM ADOQUEI,
A Grisaille

This is a demonstration of a head in grisaille. This head took 30 minutes, a quick demo to show my students how one can have a foundation for alla prima, (the direct approach to painting.) The grisaille method can take a couple of hours, sometimes days. There are different approaches to the grisaille method. There is no one better way, it often depends on the temperament and style of the artists. It is a useful skill to learn.

basic grammar that is needed to start. The rest of the experience comes automatically as the student continues to work after finishing school. It has always been this way for all good artists. There are many valuable things the student will learn on his own.

Of course, the advanced student might only use a school or a studio to sharpen up his skills; the student should not in any case think he has to get every little thing from school. No artist ever did. Some artists spend a long time at school, not because they are waiting to learn everything, but because they like the practice and the logistics. After my education in Africa, I stayed with my teacher in New York for almost seven years, until I got so busy with work that I could not afford the time to go to classes anymore. For the advanced student, it wouldn't be a bad idea to take some time off from school every now and then to see what he can do on his own. The advantages of work done by the advanced student on his own are much greater, and more appreciated by clients and gallery owners, than the advantages of work done in class. Especially figures. Because paintings done in class are exercises, they tend to have repetitious qualities.

To better understand the elements of painting, it is good for the student to experiment on his own in addition to going to class. The student might think these elements are understood in class, but not until he tries them on his own, without the assistance of his teacher or input from other students, will he know what he knows.

While the basic painting method is made up of three approaches, any other approach derives from these, as I said before. Nevertheless, if you put ten professional artists together in the same studio with the same materials, don't be surprised—you will see ten different approaches. So one can never duel in only one way, the only way the Gods, the deities and the saints approve. There is no one way of working! But for the student who is yet to find his own personal way, it is more important not to fall into a particular style that comes from some individual artist's style. Something like that can either corrupt or hinder your growth or will be too limiting for your ambitions.

The Three Basic Approaches to Painting

1) Start by drawing the entire subject with pencil or charcoal; then gradually and carefully fill in the drawing with paint.
2) Begin by doing a tonal study in grisaille, solving all tonal and compositional problems before beginning to paint in full color.
3) The Prima Coup: Start painting directly on the canvas. This very seductive style is the most deceiving style of painting; the premise is to make painting alla prima look easy to do and spontaneous. An artist's skill at drawing can make alla prima seem easy, but this often deceives the beginner, who can't tell how much skill is hidden underneath the spontaneous look. This method is also deceiving because the layman thinks it is about just painting and rushing to get finished, whereas, it is about solving complicated painting problems with economical means and capturing a moment of time as it occurs.

It takes different temperaments to master each of these techniques, and it will take some training to do all three; a complete professional can do most of these techniques—he just has to adjust his temperament accordingly. But in reality the average artist by nature can only be good in one. Often the first method is employed for big commercial projects. You plan your work, and then work the plan, solving all the problems with foundational drawing. The second method tends to combine a little bit of both the first and third methods. Luckily for me, my early training gave me a commercial background, so I was taught the first method. Then in Europe, I started learning the second method, grisaille. Again, most experienced professionals can do both the first and second, and their preference is only based on what they individually like and what is suitable for a particular subject or project. There is no one method approved by the gods, even though some artists will make it seem so. Up to a certain point in painting history, there were just a few methods, some more popular than others. The success of a master may make us sometimes believe it is the technique that made the artist, but this is wrong; it is the other way round, the artist makes and popularizes a style, a technique or a movement, but like everyone else, great masters of the classics made the technique they worked in look like that was God's chosen way to work.

So the masters of the prima coup technique can make the student feel it is the only way to paint, very seductive and engaging. Some bad practitioners can make the classic methods look too antique for modern taste; practitioners who

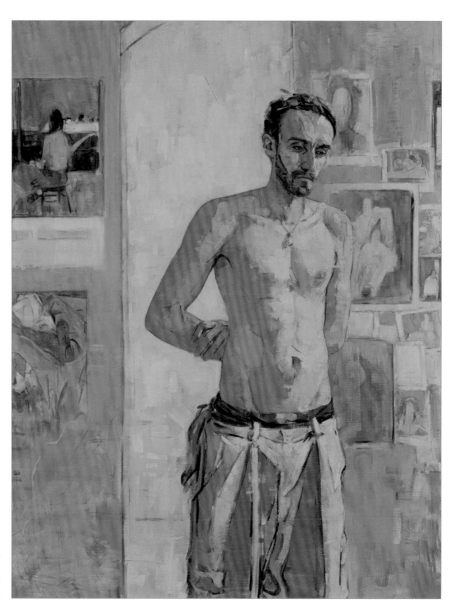

Figure 56

MARY BETH
MCKENZIE

aren't good enough can make alla prima seem to be a slap-on, insensitive way of painting. But when done well, the prima coup can make any painter jealous of the practitioner's skill. At the end of the day, learn the ABCs and the grammar, have something good to say and say it well in a simple manner. The struc-

Figure 57

SAMUEL ADOQUEI, *A Modern Workhorse in France*, oil on canvas

ture of a painting—the technique, how the message is delivered and the vision of the artist are the only things that matter. You too if you work sensitively can help popularize a new technical approach.

No one cares about Gandhi's accent, the race of Martin Luther King or the looks of Abraham Lincoln. The noble vision, how the message is delivered and the technique used are what matters. The artist's greatest ideas and visions have to be well delivered and to deliver well the artist needs good technique, not necessarily the technique approved of by the gods. In the end, the imagination of artists and how the content of that imagination can be helpful to mankind are the things that will be important. Any message, so long as it can improve our lives, will gain the approval of the masses; in return the technique will be respected.

CHAPTER ◂O11◂

IMPORTANT SUBJECTS TO LEARN

The Still Life, Portrait, Nude and Landscape

Before Vincent van Gogh became Van Gogh, everyone thought cypress trees and muddy farmers' boots were ugly.

Subject matter is the least of an art student's worries; the student should make some effort to keep it that way until he/she graduates. While still learning, it will be helpful if he or she does not encourage his or her own likes and dislikes. Having likes and dislikes will affect the student's growth and sometimes interferes with the teacher's program. No good art teacher likes to know that a student of his/hers does not think his assignments are good enough. It will be a great advantage to the student to develop a broad range of likings; the student does not know what he/she might uncover by painting a variety of subjects. Besides, the more the student understands all there is for him/her to understand in school the better it will be for that student. I was lucky to start learning early, because my teachers never had to convince me to paint anything. They just asked me to paint. It is not always like this in today's studio. Sometimes I have to convince the student that the subject is set up as a project. The choice of the right subject matter will be decided fairly by the teacher, who has experience, knowledge and broadmindedness. This compares to the inexperienced choices students would make. If due to unawareness, you have developed likes and dislikes in choosing subjects, work hard at changing in order to develop a broader outlook. If you don't, the chance of your learning well and getting the best out of yourself in a studio environment is very slim and you will develop limited skills. During my student years, I painted anything in front of me with no questions asked; my goal at that period was to paint in order to acquire a broad understanding of the craft, as well as knowledge and experience of the field.

I have had students call me up to find out what the subject matter was going to be in my still life classes before deciding if they should come to class or not. Sometimes a student walks into the studio and, if they don't like what is set up, they go out and buy flowers.   Sometimes a student will draw for a day or two and then not show up for the rest of the session. It is not healthy to develop the idea that the subject has to be inspiring in order to paint it. On the contrary, art has to bring out the inspiration hidden in things.

STILL LIFE PAINTING:

The Easiest Way to Master Painting Technique

How Still Life Objects Got Their Identity
(Written and edited by Still Life students)

This past weekend, we painted still life arrangements that Sam had put together of some of the largest beets I had ever seen, plus onions, small potatoes and quinces. As he often does towards the end of a Saturday or Sunday painting session, Sam told all of us to bring our paintings out into the hallway. The paintings were arranged for viewing, three or four at a time. We students gathered round to get a good view and hear what Sam had to say about what we had done.

Sam began by encouraging us to look critically at the paintings. He started with the basics like composition and light effects and encouraged us to evaluate how each of the painters had achieved those (or not). Then, he moved to questions about the quinces. He asked if we could recognize the quinces as quinces. Indeed, most of the time, it was hard to tell whether a quince was a quince, or a lemon or a pear or some other round object in the students' pictures. I thought sure that Sam would follow this quince/no quince observation with some words about basic shapes and planes. I can never look at a pear again without thinking of what Sam once said about the shoulders of a pear—that plane that sits where

Figure 58 SAM ADOQUEI, *Apples, Grapes and Butterfly Plant, oil on canvas*

the cone-like part of the pear meets the sphere-like part. But no, Sam did not go
to basic shapes and planes. He went to the Angel Gabriel.

Sam told an origin story for still life painting. He took us back to the
beginning when God was putting the final touches on his earthly creations. The
Angel Gabriel was a kind of site manager sent to earth to insure that all the
details were right. He returned with a report for God that a little more work
was required. Angel Gabriel observed that God had created so many different
kinds of objects, such an amazing array of different fruits and vegetables. But
people on earth were behaving as if there were only a few types. Men and
women were missing the distinctiveness, lumping things together, and failing to
appreciate the uniqueness of each kind of fruit and vegetable. Angel Gabriel

Figure 59

JEANETTE
CHRISTJANSEN,
Former Miss Denmark

was especially moved by the blind man who failed to notice, until he bit into it, that the tart fruit was not the sweet fruit that he thought it was. Angel Gabriel decided that people could be helped tremendously if God enhanced the differences in form and texture between different fruits and vegetables. He convinced God of how much better it would be if the lemon and lime had bumpy skin—so different from the smooth, paper-like texture of the onion, and then if the lime were made more round and the lemon more oval, even someone who couldn't see colors could tell them apart. Upgrading the quince was especially important. So, God gave it that special dimple at the top, attached a little cone shape over its large faceted sphere, and put all that fuzz on its skin. God wanted people never again to mistake a quince for a pear. He took a pear and put a little peak at the top where the fruit meets the stem, gave it a larger and slimmer cone than that of the quince, and blessed it with a smooth skin.

It is the job of the still life painter to be true to Angel Gabriel's mission. The painter needs to be sensitive to and record all of that uniqueness and difference that God was moved to give to the fruits and vegetables.

Analysis

Even though the artist brings his inherent and unique artistic style and personality, and uses distinctive materials, to create his art, it is how he sees and observes, and the vision he has, that makes his art and his artistic self different from that of other artists.

The evolution of how the student sees and observes nature will depend on the sensitivities he develops at school; an apple should not look like a tomato, just as Cynthia should not look like Agnes. Writers can experiment with new words but they do not have to use wrong spelling and incorrect grammar in order to be different from their peers and predecessors. The way an artist portrays the natural world around him is his contribution to society and the contribution depends on which part or side of nature he likes and decides to portray and bring forth. The differences between artists always come down to the technique (language) used, the vision and the contribution.

It is a lame argument for the student to make that by painting things realistically, the way they appear in nature, he will lose his personality. It is through responding to, studying and imitating nature, that the artist learns his craft and finds himself.

Still Life Painting

Years ago an outraged student confronted me to say that she had not paid so much tuition to paint a glass and an apple. She didn't understand that the subject was set up as a study in reds, spheres, transparency and textures. Even though I had explained the reasons for setting up the subject, she still expressed the opinion that she wanted to paint a subject of her own choice. I have seen students who cannot paint simple objects trying anxiously to paint double figure poses. Imagine. In the history of art I have never heard of a studio exercise in which any great artist does double figures in his beginning phase. The attitude that one must paint what one wants to or paint what inspires one is a therapeutic approach. It has cost students more years of frustration, agony and tuition than anything else. You will need the knowledge you acquire in painting simple things for future complicated problems. A painting project should be a problem-solving project.

If you think of painting more complex subjects one day, then a simple change in attitude toward what subject you prefer might be all you need to make the next jump to mastering your technical problems. Enjoy the process of painting; step back and examine yourself. Learn to paint simple objects using spheres, cones, cylinders and cubes with concave and convex effects, also wedges and different textures, and apply this knowledge to the subjects you encounter. All natural things are built up of these simple basic shapes. Almost all of us in the beginning of our studies think that painting difficult and complicated things will make us better.

PORTRAIT PAINTING

The student should have noble feelings towards people—
passion and sentiment. Also, he needs a logical
and analytical approach to drawing.

It doesn't require any special talent to learn to paint portraits but it does requires a well-trained knowledgeable talent to create beautiful, creative portraits that aren't just renditions of faces but are artworks. Portraiture is the ideal branch of painting, so the student should pay careful attention to learn to paint

Figure 60

SAMUEL ADOQUEI,
A Family, Monbos,
Bergerac, oil on
canvas

portraits well. There is always a demand for portraits; someone is always willing to pay to have a portrait done of himself, a family member or a loved one. Portrait painting is very demanding and can be approached from several angles commercially. Portraits by Picasso or Matisse are very philosophical. Cézanne and some of the Impressionists have a more personal touch, while Sargent's portraits have both of the above qualities. It would not be totally wrong to say his work has a commercial touch because a higher percentage of his work was meant to satisfy the sitter. Van Gogh's work also falls into several categories but his works are more personal than commercial. Because of these differences in approach the student can become confused and lose his focus on what are the important things to learn as a portrait artist, or how to go about learning it. To the student, portraits can mean capturing a likeness of the one who commissioned the work or capturing the soul and character of a certain particular individual.

A portrait can be just a mechanical copy or rendition of a head or it could be a study of an individual in his environment with the artist having to deal with all that implies. It is because the artist has to master all these complexities that makes most portrait painters more versatile as painters in general than a landscape painter might be. All great painters of the past were also great portrait painters, but not necessarily all portrait painters are or will become great creative artists. Creativity and craft are different. By the time the serious artist has mastered all the complexities it takes to be able to create good portraits, the artist has indirectly developed other important artistic skills as well as his talent and temperament.

No matter how the artist approaches painting portraits, the results that he achieves have more to do with who the artist is than who the subject is. The artist cannot produce a mere shallow image of someone if the artist himself is a sensitive, thoughtful, caring and nature-loving human being, It cannot capture a sensitive, touching expression of an individual if he is a shallow, cold insensitive person. What the artist creates is a result of his taste, temperament, knowledge and experience. The negative reputation portrait painters have of being the same as commercial artists who just paint faces is caused by the artists themselves who never broaden their talent beyond portraiture. It is neither the subject nor the business of portraiture that forces the artist to be mediocre, rather it is the artist who never had any vision beyond copying faces, or never took time off to develop his taste, sense of beauty and creative sensibilities, in learning to

Figure 61

SAMUEL ADOQUEI,
Untitled, oil on canvas

Painted during my student years, circa 1990.

paint portraits. The tradional principle that believes technique is everything can also suppress other unique talents the artist has. The artist becomes a good technician who paints like everyone else but looses his personal and unique characteristics.

For art students, the biggest mistake is the tendency to put so much importance and emphasis on the head and its features that they never allow themselves the opportunity to learn other important elements in portraiture, like the handling of how the props are intertwined into the background.

Technically, portraiture and figure painting are the most difficult and demanding of all the areas of specialization in painting—so the student needs to be very dedicated, focused and willing to work hard. There are three types of portraiture the student should be aware of in order to make sure he learns the right one.

Commercial portraiture (realistic portraits) is the kind of painting in which the artist is not the one with the last say or approval. The customer is always right and no matter how good the portrait painter is, the customer always holds the upper hand and always has the last say. The student should first understand the reason the customer holds the upper hand; the customer commissions the work and he is the one paying for it. He is paying because he wants to acquire a work that satisfies his artistic desires. If the student or the artist wants the customer's money, then the artist has to satisfy the customer.

Creative portraiture is an area of portraiture where the artist does what he wishes for the sake of achieving a certain image that he sees in his mind's eye or a certain look that he wishes to share with the public. The artist adds to or adjusts the features in order to reach this goal. The artist decides why he paints a certain head, how he wants to paint it and what kind of message he wants to convey with the head. The artist therefore paints from life and all sorts of references but he may twist, change or exaggerate what he sees to say what he wishes.

Imaginative portraiture (sometimes personal) describes a portrait that often comes from a real person but may come from memory. A made-up face is a kind of fantasy face that the artist imagines. It can include car-toons or be realistic yet it is created only on the basis of an image that the artist envisions.

Figure 62

TWO HOUR PORTRAIT PAINTING DEMONSTRATION

Figure one and Figure two are Illustrations of early stages of portrait painting method, the technic of blocking in with local colors and light and shade. the artist concentrating on Values, Light and Color. This stage helps and strengthens the student's ablities to mix and capture the true flesh tone of an individual, it is the standard method for the imprssionistic approach to painting.

Most professional artists who can paint heads and faces have the skill and temperament to go back and forth between painting commercial and creative portraits.

No matter what the student's preferences are, it is the duty of the art student to consider what is at stake: talent, tuition and the limited time available to learn the basics. By learning to paint accurate resemblances of people, the artist acquires the skill to paint imaginative heads and faces and to create cartoons or faces that he likes. So the student shouldn't get too involved with all the philosophical, psychological and stylized aspects of portraiture. The student should learn the art and science of painting portraits, then divert those skills to the branch of portraiture he wishes to specialize in. There are several great portrait painters whose work might not only inspire and influence students interested in portrait painting but also help them to really understand the science of portraiture.

Frans Hals's and Hans Holbein's portraits are ideal examples of work to aspire to. They are truthful, clear, precise and more explicable in technique and in the handling of problem solving, yet done artistically; their directness forces

the student to understand what is expected of a portrait painter. Other Old Master portraits are painted in a way new students might find difficult to understand. Also, Frans Hals and Hans Holbein represent opposite ends of oil painting technique. They have extremely different characters and temperaments yet both painted all kinds of portraits. Frans Hals was a master of the rapid spontaneous technique of finishing a painting in a single sitting, while Hans Holbein was an amazing master of the slow, careful, step-by-step technique that employed careful planning. Holbein used a method that required drawing the subject first, and then transferring the drawing to a canvas followed by careful painting, building layer upon layer of paint, to create the desired effect.

For survival or commercial advantage, the artist can technically learn both extremes, the technique of Frans Hals and that of Hans Holbein (or similiarly, that of Jean-August-Dominque Ingres), but it is not worth the trouble to do so because acquiring the techniques and temperaments needed to master them both requires a long period of time, and then they contradict each other most of the time anyway. But more importantly, the artist's success will depend on how well he uses what he knows.

To the average student, whose vision is to do work that society may gain from, it might sound necessary to learn both ways of working, especially because the means are there, and the teachers are accessible and affordable, but then again knowing every technique or style should not be the goal of the student, rather he should strive to understand some basic, effective and clear way of solving technical problems.

If the student lets go of his likes and dislikes, he will sooner or later, with his open mindedness, gravitate towards the kind of style that suits his temperament.

Besides all these subtleties, the student will gain much from class that will help him concentrate on understanding the mechanics of painting portraits.

One would think that in order to draw cartoons, the artist needs no formal training. All the artist needs is a convincing talent. But almost any cartoon studio requires their artists to draw well and artists interested in this field should have very good training in drawing figures and portraits. Understanding portraits and figures broadens the advantages the student has should he decide to pursue any field in the arts. Any art director is aware that any artist who draws well and has formal training can be trained to do anything. This is mainly because several parts of our senses get developed automatically as we learn to

Figure 63

SAMUEL ADOQUEI,
*Portrait, oil on
canvas*

*This is a classic exam-
ple of portrait sample.
the student who
desires to pursue por-
trait commissions has
to have several por-
trait samples. the sam-
ples display the artist's
technique, style and
vision.*

draw portraits and figures: our sense of concentration; our mathematical or analytical sense; our personal love and respect for nature; and our ability to see
each individual as a unique respectful entity.

FIGURE PAINTING

The figure is the most complicated subject to paint; for students several things have to go right in order to create a good figurative drawing or painting. If, for the student's first attempt at doing the figure, he has an experienced artist to guide him, then that is fine. In the beginning, students will find it useful to do some copying from any reference source (photos and magazines as well as drawing books). Before taking any courses, copying has always been the natural way to start drawing the figure, copying will allow the student to get some idea of what it takes to do the figure well. It will also prepare the student's mind for the analytical process he will have to go through in order to achieve good proportions. It also gives the student a chance to work at his own pace. At first, it's a good idea for the new student to start drawing some still life objects or cast sculptures before attempting the life model. The live model is very difficult and to start drawing straight from the model can be very frustrating. Often, the first three months will prove be a waste of the student's time.

The early months are best spent and more fulfilling if the student avoids the life model and only works on drawing objects in the studio: spherical objects and cubical objects and fabrics and then gradually moves on to the life model with the help of the teacher. Beginning students who try to draw directly from the life model, skipping the study of plaster casts and copying, as well as that of drawing still lifes, will face frustration most of the time.

When drawing from life the student has to learn to see the abstract shapes that make up the complete figure. This is a way of seeing that experienced teachers can explain better than written texts can; such a teacher's help will make it easy to solve the problems of the parts of the figure, for example. A tree, for instance, is first seen as a big oval or triangular shape and then divided into the massive foliage against the trunk (upper and lower), then the forms are divided into branches followed by twigs if necessary. The figure is also first divided into the upper and lower torso and then the limbs followed by the eyes, nose and fingers. Sometimes I see students doing well with a technique that allows them to work from within (the inside-out technique). The inside-out technique allows the student to start with a section of the figure and then gradually, little by little, develop the whole figure by developing the drawing from that small part outwards. I find this inside-out technique is a method suitable to certain temperaments. It is worth learning after the student has mastered the basic constructional approach. In general, to achieve desirable results, all other techniques come from the main basic approach described above. The student first has to learn to simplify or unify all the complicated parts of the figure by looking for a few simple abstract shapes that, when combined, make up the whole figure. This method of using simple geometric shapes for constructing the figure makes it easier to relate the different parts of the figure to each other in order to figure out the figure's basic proportions. Only when the student is satisfied with how the overall proportions of the whole figure look when compared to the parts can he proceed to tackle planes, light source, details and character study. Often the impatient student will want to rush to achieve realistic results or to set down details. It is this impatient habit that pressures the beginner to jump over the methodical process that leads to achieving correct proportions. Knowing the method described above and habitually applying it helps the student to master the technique of life drawing.

The thought behind this construction is based on the idea that the whole is always bigger than the sum of its parts. Therefore, if the beginning student can get the bigger shapes down correctly he will find it easy to locate details; in other words, the details will fit into place if the whole is correct. On the other hand, no amount of good detail will save an incorrect whole.

It is only useful to study anatomy after a student has learned all that there is to know about the constructional method of drawing, when he has confidently trained his natural abilities—his eye, mind and hand co-ordination and gained some instruction in figure drawing. Even Leonardo had to learn anatomy when and only when he knew enough and wanted to explore and specialize in the figure. It is only when a student has mastered the basics and become an advanced student who can draw very well that basic artistic anatomy is necessary. There have been many great masters from the past, from almost all cultures, that have produced artistically great works that have added to the development of our civilization who never studied anatomy. Thinking that anatomy lessons are necessary or the only way to approach the figure is a modern phenomenon. It is only when the advanced student knows what he is doing and what he wants as an artist, that is, when he knows what direction he wants to specialize in as an artist, that he can benefit from taking a course in artistic anatomy or learning it from books.

Figure 64

SAMUEL ADOQUEI, *Green Kimono, oil on canvas*

First, learn and understand masses and shapes by using angles to compare them to each other as a way to solve basic proportional problems. In the beginning stages of using the constructional method, the results often look rigid and not as elegant as the layman wishes, but out of these rigid results, artists often find their own personal style, method or technique, one that suits their personal taste and temperament. Therefore, by learning it, the potential art student is guaranteed to find himself too. Until the artist has learned the basic approach and has acquired a methodical and habitual approach to solving drawing problems, it will not be wise for him to attempt such areas of drawing as anatomy or even gesture drawing, etc. These will be of no use to students and will hold them back. They won't be able to comprehend these methods. Getting used to incorrect approaches may get in the way of the student's understanding of the

Figure 65

JEANETTE
CHRISTJANSEN,
*Still Life (Pot, Bottle
and Vegetables)*

right approach.

No Old Master that I have read about started learning anatomy straight away before learning the basics of EYE, MIND and HAND coordination. (Which means learning the natural way to draw well without any mechanical devices by training the natural analytical senses through comparing and measuring.) The ambitious student with many expectations might find the basics stiff, sometimes slow and difficult to master, but he should stick to it, because they are the most logical, fundamental and practical skills to learn. Do whatever it takes to avoid being tempted into learning how to make stylized attractive drawings. Find an instructor with the experience, knowledge and patience to teach this method and work as hard as you can to find the means of learning it. It is the most valuable, broad, progressive method for drawing, and it is very reliable once the student understands the process.

To grow and pursue whatever the artist's visions are it is first necessary to acquire this reliable technical approach for achieving results, then the artist can move on and experiment or innovate as he wishes. Be cautious of attractive, stylized and addictive styles that suit the temperament of few artists. Sometimes the impatient, discontented student in a hurry to surpass the great Old Masters and outdo him/herself will get attracted to drawings made for exhibition—to styles, effects and looks that offer instant gratification but don't have enough structure and substance to fall back on when the artist is out of school and facing more complicated drawing problems. Often these styles are not general enough in their application to allow the artist the freedom to explore and find himself. The rewards of learning the figure are unlimited, mainly because of all it takes to understand it. It is one of those experiences that by the time you finish learning it, all of your other senses have so much improved that the experience can be applied to other technical branches of art. Even if the student does not like painting the figure, this tremendous benefit alone should convince him to consider studying how to understand the figure.

The benefits of learning the figure include improvement of the analytical and mathematical senses and the handling of textures (gained from painting hair, skin and nails). Learning figure painting also contributes to the student's knowledge of objects in atmosphere as well as understanding the figure in its surroundings, plus such details as dealing with edges. Other benefits include learning to use figures in compositions, such as landscapes, interiors, groups of figures and portraits.

LANDSCAPE PAINTING

The student's biggest misconception about the art of landscape painting is not thinking it is serious or difficult enough to give it the time, attention and sensitivity that is necessary to understand the technical process involved. This kind of mindset is the reason why most painters do not have the right knowledge, sensitivity and desire to paint decent landscapes. Compared to portraiture, students always underrate landscape painting; therefore they do not develop the right attitude and temperament towards the subject.

Until the student finds someone who is very good at painting landscape, whom he can paint side-by-side with and pick up some pointers from, it is worth finding an experienced and knowledgeable landscape painter who is teaching the subject and spend some summers outdoors learning landscape painting. In the beginning, the student should avoid painting or learning landscape from photographs. The faults he picks up from painting from photos will be too costly in the long run. The rules of landscape painting are the same as those in portraiture and the figurative arts. Landscape painting can be divided into realistic or impressionistic landscape, idealistic landscape and imaginary or fantasy landscape. It is more beneficial to the student to spend his learning period studying how to paint in a realistic manner. Learning anything other than the rules, techniques and principles of painting landscapes realistically will not be worth the student's investment. In landscape painting, it is more helpful and important for the student to learn the realistic or constructive approach to painting from nature. Going outdoors and painting from life is not only the most fun but also the most instructive way to begin; once understood, all other approaches will become easy to learn.

After school, the student will be able to follow his own personal preferences in choosing the style in which he wants to work, but before then the lessons that he will get from painting outdoors are the ideal lessons for everyone who wants to paint landscape.

After school, there will always be lots of room for exploration and experimentation. While studying, the student should familiarize himself with the great landscape masters of the past and present. For example, Corot, Monet, Cézanne, Poussin and George Inness are all worth studying, as is John Constable. These great masters are from different traditions and from different times and backgrounds, but they all did wonderful landscapes. The student cannot go wrong having them as inspirational models to emulate. There are many other artists who also painted landscapes, but with these names any student will find a style suitable to his taste.

Landscape, like the figure or portrait, when taken seriously, can be approached in unlimited ways, each time achieving wonderful results and the work need never look like that of another artist.

In Western Art there have been many great masters specializing in landscape. Yet the experienced artist of today can still do as many wonderful things as he wishes without having to copy someone else's style. Landscape is a broad field, as challenging as any other field of art and learning it is worthy of the

same attention and dedication. The student in
the early stages of his learning won't know what
style or approach he might one day like, so he needs
to have an explorative mind if he wishes to learn and
enjoy the field. Knowing how to do landscape painting also offers a break from studio exercises, broad-
ening the way the artist sees nature. In the eyes of an
experienced landscape painter, the most ordinary
scene can become the most beautiful image.

From a commercial standpoint, landscape paintings are more accessible and are therefore easier to
sell. Also, landscapes are more readily acquired by
art enthusiasts than portraits. From a creative point
of view, landscape allows the artist the freedom to
experience and explore new subject matter and to
broaden his scope and areas of expertise. Since the

Figure 66

LANDSCAPE PAINTING DEMONSTRATION

*Illustrations of early stages of landscape paint-
ing method, the technic of blocking in with local
colors in light and shade. the artist concentrating
on Values, Light and Color, (arrangement in
color, arrangement in values, lines, shapes, texture)   This stage helps and strengthens the student's ablities to mix and capture the true colors
of nature, it is the area where structure and
design of painting are built on, the most basic yet
the important stage of landscape painting. It is
so basic that most students take it for granted.
It is this underlined structure and foundation that
makes successful landscapes communicate their
message. In this stage a complex subject can be
broken down into a couple of simplified abstract
shapes.*

appeal of landscapes is greater to both clients and gallery owners, an artist who
can paint beautiful and sensitive landscapes will find that there is always a
need for his work. Try to learn all the basic rules of landscape before graduating from school, because it is too difficult to learn on your own.

There are several technical approaches to handling landscape. Yet all the
styles or approaches always fall under the realistic approach, the idealistic
approach, the impressionistic approach or the imaginary and creative approach.
Many great painters have painted masterpieces under one or two of these

Figure 67 SAMUEL ADOQUEI, *An Old Tree in Central Park, oil on canvas*

Figure 68 SAMUEL ADOQUEI, *Portrait of My Friend Rodney*

approaches or styles but, of all of them, the impressionistic approach is the broadest. The impressionistic manner of painting trains the artist's temperament to have versatility and to be able to use other styles; it allows the artist freedom to choose other styles or approaches without prejudice. For example, it is easier for an artist to make a shift from impressionistic ways of working to realistic or idealistic or imaginary than it is to change from idealistic and imaginary to impressionism. This is because within the approach of impressionism there are many skills that the artist develops that are compatible with other approaches.

Figure 69 USHA SHARMA

Figure 70 SAMUEL ADOQUEI, *Iris and Peonies*

CHAPTER ◄012◄

THE BEAUTY AND IMPORTANCE OF COLOR

Color

Ideally, everything to be learned about color can be divided into a handful of topics: color theory, which consists of how the color wheel (color spectrum) works; learning to see the true colors of nature (the natural and intuitive way to use color); the impressionistic and expressionistic approaches to color; and the idealistic way to use color. It is worthwhile to explore all the theories that have been written on the subject. As long as the student makes sure he does not get confused about what he is being taught, becoming familiar with several theories always help. The student might not comprehend the theories in the beginning of his art education. Theories such as understanding how the color wheel works; color harmony; color analogies; complementary colors, etc. Color theory is easier to comprehend when the student has already had some practice in using and mixing colors as well as after he has gained an understanding of primary, secondary and tertiary colors.

The student can learn all the theories and principles of color on his own but the practical knowledge, mastering how to see color and how to mix color, how to use and balance color requires an advanced colorist to monitor and guide the student's approach. Therefore, the student should do whatever it takes to learn how to see color and how to mix the colors of nature and how to combine and balance them through a practical problem-solving approach. The student should find a professional colorist who is good at these things. If the student can see the true colors of nature and mix exactly what he sees, then the major areas of color problems will be solved. If not, the student should develop seeing color through his own prism, even if he has problems in seeing. Artistically, there is no such thing as color blindness. but artists have different and unique ways of seeing color.

Students should always be careful with the idealistic approach to color. The idealistic approach is an individual's personal approach and could hinder the student's development. It is more important in the beginning to develop the natural approach by trying to mix the true colors of nature. Often teachers will first make sure the student is aware of the color spectrum. The basics of color theory include: primary, secondary and tertiary colors, as well as color harmony. Most bookstores have books on how the color wheel works. The most important thing of all is composing with colors; seeing and mixing require a different kind of training than learning color theory. The teacher has to have lots of experience in painting from life; seeing and mixing the true colors of nature without exaggeration is very important. Exaggerations of color often make artworks look and feel unrealistic, chromatic and garish.

COLOR AND PAINT HANDLING
(Food for Thought)

Titian, Monet, Ingres and Matisse are all great artists in their own right who have each gained a reputation as being masters of color, yet when one puts their paintings next to each other, one will wonder how they can differ so much in everything: in style, in color, in approach and technique and in skill and often in their choice of subject matter as well as in their vision. Even though they used the same materials, their works are extremely different; one wonders what gives them the title of masters of color.

How one sees and how one uses color by mixing or arranging it, these are the ways in which these great artists differ from each other and through which they have established the styles that made their names. Since this book is more about what is necessary for the student to learn, I will leave detailed analytical theories about who they are or how each of them painted aside in order to focus on their open-mindedness, which freed them to adopt a new tradition. It is that open-mindedness that the student should cultivate. It is that open mind that separates the innovative artist from ordinary artists. It is through this open-mind-

Figure 71 NORIL SAWAKA, *Sawaka's Palette with a 5 minute demo on how I approach color*

edness that the student can adopt or emulate the manner in which these great artists went about developing. They didn't have fixed ideas; they weren't so rigid that they couldn't see beyond their own skills. The student should concentrate on what and why to study in order to acquire general skills so that he too can, in the future, develop his own personal style.

There are a number of instructors teaching nowadays, who have mastered color and its theories, natural, intuitive and scientific. It is not going to be difficult for the student to find one. Hopefully, the student is aware of how useful it is to know color; he will learn enough in his advanced period to acquire broad and general principles in hopes of having the necessary knowledge to pursue the path he or she wishes to follow. The student should also be aware that too much broadmindedness doesn't make him spread his focus too thin, so that he is trying to do everything. Luckily for me, I studied at a school where teaching

art was more the teaching of a craft, so the student got to learn and practice all these different theories. It was only after I left school that I started to realize that my taste leans towards realism and impressionism. It was more important for me to use colors and paint as a tool or a vehicle rather than worrying about which style I want to paint in.

Unfortunately, in recent times, extreme beliefs about what is right and what is wrong, or which tradition is the chosen tradition, can force a student to choose one tradition over another instead of learning basic skills and leaving the choices for the future. It's an attitude of either Cézanne or Ingres. The student is left with a choice of having to choose one tradition and turn his nose up at other approaches, ways of thinking and working. It is often only when the student leaves school and is willing to expand his mind that he can start on his own to search again for broader beliefs. It is then that he goes on to search for an experienced colorist to learn color from.

In general, we have come a long way toward understanding and using color since the times of cave and fresco painting to those of Matisse and Andy Warhol.

Methods of Paint Handling

Oil paints, unlike other mediums, are very versatile. They can be used to create unlimited and unimaginable effects and illusions, from the most delicate, faint, film-like effect to the strongest sculptural effect, creating a soft atmospheric illusion or one of an impenetrable flatness. While one artist likes to apply thin layer over thin layer, another works with a palette knife to achieve a thickness greater than one inch. In some instances, the artist's taste doesn't permit brush-strokes to show in the final work while another artist's taste and temperament

Figure 72

SAMUEL ADOQUEI,
Study of Flesh Tones,
oil on canvas

Painted as a
demonstration for
American Artist
Magazine.

prefers to show every single mark. There are some artists who fall in between these extremes; they allow the subject to determine when to use thin layers of paint and when to use thick strokes to achieve the necessary effects. I see painting technique as a language that the artist uses to achieve his ends so I fall in between the two extremes. It is in between the two extremes that most artists eventually find their unique personal language. This evolution happens smoothly if the artist has been given a broad and general foundation to start with. It is a matter of developing his skills so that the student can work from the very thinnest paint to the thickest paint, skills that have survival advantages for the young artist's career.

Some instructors are very good at working in the personal style they have

Figure 73 SUZANNE OUELLETTE, *Shoes, oil on canvas*

developed over the years—they've worked hard at mastering this unique personal style. While the student needs to respect such styles, they may not be suitable for his education and may even hinder it. The student should just make sure that such a unique personal style will not confuse him at the time of his life when he should be learning a more general approach. From Giotto to Van Gogh, there have been masters who have appeared out of every kind of painting background, the lean and thin as well as the thick and chunky. The goal of the student is to be equipped with the general basics of solving painting problems, and to be broadminded and respectful of other traditions and to acknowledge their contributions.

If, in studying art, we remove our likes and dislikes regarding how materials are used, we realize how many great and wonderful artists have come from different schools and backgrounds. There have been many great masters and great artworks from every tradition. It is not the manner or style in which an artist works that makes the artist, it is the artist's mind, accomplishment and vision that make some styles, or traditions, more important than others. Only with hindsight, and from hearing such romantic stories as that of Vincent Van Gogh who ended up becoming a successful artist, do the painters of today want to live and work like Van Gogh or the other impressionists did. We go to museums and want to be like an artist we don't know. Had we lived in their time, would we too despise them and laugh at them?

Color has come a long way since the time when the public had just a handful of colors on their palette, when even what people wore fell within a limited color range.

CHAPTER ◂013◂

COMPOSITION IS EVERYTHING

What Is Composition and Why Is it Important?

Composition in its simplest and truest form is the art of arranging the elements of a given subject so that the viewer can respond to the picture the way the artist intended. Therefore, the artist's intention should be to make an artwork that delivers to the subconscious mind of the viewer his message, whether it be concerned with beauty, mood or politics. This is achieved by a well thought out, calculated arrangement, whose intentional (or accidental) effects are achieved by creating illusions. Grasping the value of composition—achieving a natural, intuitive understanding of its importance—is the most important attitude the student can acquire. The student should religiously accept the important role of composition in painting and all other arts.

In pictures, we respond first to the pictorial elements, such as line, shape, color, value and texture. How these elements are balanced (their edges, movement, space or juxtaposition within each artwork) is what makes us respond to pictures. In composing, the artist has to know the natural law of opposites (in color, line, shape, value, size and texture). It is a compositional law that suggests that a message in an artwork will be more effective if things are balanced with their opposites. For example, any large object will look larger if it has something very small next to it. A bright color will seem brighter if the colors juxtaposed to it are dull. A round shape will seem rounder if it has an object next to it that is angular. The concept is the same in real life, good and bad, dry and wet. It is more obvious in the theater and is one of Shakespeare's strengths in composing his plots. The law of opposites, as a compositional device, is well worth exploring for the advanced student.

Thick paint against thin and bright against dull. Big shapes against small. The artist who desires to compose well, to break nature down into this way of seeing, has to put himself in the viewer's shoes. A banana from a distance is just a yellowish cylindrical bent thing, but from up close the viewer will respond to the banana. A black shape on a lighter background will draw more attention than the same black object on a darker background. If the viewer sees the banana differently than what the artist intended then it is the fault of the artist for not being able to use the right device to communicate well with the viewer. A fresh apple, if painted badly, can come across as a rotten apple or a nude model if not composed well might look like a naked model. The same idea applies to writing. "My husband has a dog" when written should never be read as "My husband is a dog." The writer will only be forgiven if the reader perceives him as lame or inefficient with the language or if the writer has the opportunity to explain himself to whoever reads the sentence, a very impossible task, explaining one's self all the time. These inefficiencies of communication are the main purpose of learning some do's and don'ts in the creative field.

In order to create effective compositions, the artist has to imagine how the average viewer sees artworks or how the artist himself wants the viewer to look

Figure 74 (above)

RICHARD MULLER, *Etching of night scene*

This is a good example of composition in values.

Figure 75 (above right)

SAMUEL ADOQUEI, *From My Room at Bob Alexander's House, Overlooking Little Venice, London, graphite drawing*

at the work. Doing this can often give the innovative artist some freedom to explore and discover ways of solving problems or indirectly controlling the psyche of the viewer and his senses.

There are some theories, as well as some do's and don'ts, that are worth exploring for the advanced student. Learning them will make problem solving easier. There are several scientific formulas. Different traditions believe in different theories, so it is best, first of all, to understand how important composition is and then develop an interest in it. For starters, make it a point to let your teacher help you with it. The more interested you are in it the more likely your teacher will spend the time it takes to help you understand. During your advanced years at school, research and learn as much about composition theories as possible.

One of the goals in this chapter is to let you know how important composition is, so the advanced student will take it very seriously and pay attention to it as he paints figures, portraits, landscapes and still lifes. All in all, it pays for the advanced student to develop the belief that composition is everything. It takes as much time to master the skills involved in composing as it takes to learn drawing. This belief is based on the fact that composition comes first in

Figure 76

SIGMUND ABELES,
Self Portrait with
Horse Skull

letting the viewer move around the picture by attracting him into it. Then to hold the viewer's attention through the subject matter before delivering the message. Failure to accept this belief or idea will lead to works that have to rely on an idea to deliver the true intended message or else will deliver the wrong message or a different message than the artist intended. The student will have to learn to be a good draftsman and to think like a decorator. He must juggle the elements of composition in order to get his message across. The desire to subconsciously believe fully in the importance of composition will in return develop the interest to always think of it when starting a painting.

In the anatomy of a painting, the role composition plays is as important as all the other elements put together. Many excellently painted pictures have failed to be recognized because they lacked the factors that attract and engage the viewer. The more attractive and engaging a painting is the more successful and memorable it will be, and the easier it will be for the message to hit its target.

Before a student makes the jump from being an advanced student to the professional environment, he should give composition the same attention as he gave to the rest of the factors in painting. And the student should also make it a point to understand the theories and the art and science of composing. How a work is viewed, understood, received and accepted depends on the artist's use of the compositional elements.

The will to get your artworks engraved in the subconscious mind of the viewer is served by making sure the work travels to the mind through the eyes. This is something only the device of composition can do well.

Henry Matisse on Composition-
What I dream of is an art of balance, of purity and serenity, devoid of troubling or depressing subject matter, an art which could be for every mental worker, for the businessman as well as the man of letters, for example, a soothing, calming influence on the mind, something like a good armchair which provides relaxation from physical fatigue. Henry Matisse ("Notes of a Painter," Published in December 1908)

Such an advice is a jewel for all advancing artists, any student of composition. It is always the reasons behind the mind of great artists that the advancing artist can learn from. Not the works they produce.

THE IMPORTANCE OF COMPOSITION

Three Stages of Composition

Composition can make or break a painting. Composition helps clarify the message the artist wants to convey to the viewer. But composition, like other subjects, needs to be planned out well if it is to be successful. A painting's message goes through several stages before it becomes clear and understood.

Stage One: First, the artist conceives of a particular idea/message.

Stage Two: Then, he plans the execution of the idea so that his true vision will be the final result. Planning is based on a selection of those elements that make an artwork successful on the two-dimensional surface.

Stage Three: Carrying out the plan. A successful message is achieved because the artist has used all the elements of composition to help clarify the image in his mind's eye. Behind every great successful painting there is an artist with an understanding of the laws of composition who has used those laws in such a way that the viewer looks at the work long enough for the message to sneak into his subconscious mind.

For any artwork to be successful, it has to have all the elements that make such a work visually pleasing for a long period of time. If there is an important message in the work, the viewer won't miss it. First and most importantly is that composition play a major role. The way a picture is painted is the second important thing that keeps us involved with the painting. Whether we stay for couple of minutes or just a moment to look at an artwork will depend on how the composition and the technique engage us. After this the message will either become a memorable image or just a flash. In all viewing situations, the longer we stay looking at pictures, the more likely they will become part of us. No matter how grand the idea behind the work, if the viewer is not forced by compositional strategies to keep looking, the painting will just become another picture.

The other important purpose of composition, besides being visually pleasing, is to lead the viewer cunningly to the message of the artwork. The way each artist leads his viewer to the message is where the art of composition lies.

Figure 77 SAMUEL ADOQUEI, *Peaches and Roses, oil on canvas*

The artist can excite the viewer to grasp the message—by means of drama, line, value, shape and color as well as how the edges are handled. The artist can also guide the viewer gently to the message, by means of the subtle arrangement of all the elements above.

The artist can also force the message on the viewer by means of choking him with the message. The "shock value" approach is the opposite of sneaking the message into the subconscious of the viewer. Sometimes the subject matter plays a part in how it is portrayed and sometimes the kind of following the artist intends to attract also predicts what sort of compositional strategy the artist should use. For example, the works that Albrecht Dürer created for the masses are very different in their compositional approach from that of the more personal works he made for the few.

Human beings, sophisticated by nature, with time tend to despise things we have been choked with. On the other hand, humans accept and remember messages that come to them slowly and register in their subconscious. For these reasons, the student should be cautious about using effects that shock.

These strategic ways of making sure a message reaches its target depend on personal preferences and temperaments and on whether the intent of the artist is to shock or to guide gently or to sneak up on his audience. It is the artist's own personal decision. For the student, the important goal is to learn all aspects of com- position. There is no one

Figure 78 CHRISTOPHER BROWN

way and there are many theories. Some instructors think composition is an intuitive subject and should be taught from a personal point of view, others believe otherwise. They believe that composition is a scientific subject and the student should understand that there are principles that when followed will always give good results. These objective rules and the science of composing are part of the legacy we have inherited from the past. This legacy includes theories left by various ancient cultures from around the globe. In the west it comes from the Greeks and the Old Masters of Western Art. All cultures have their own compositional principles. And one can't say which are better. Students should just learn first what they are being taught. Each instructor believes in the kind of theories that work for him. For myself, I have studied every theory and principle I could get my hands on. No matter what schools and ideas you follow, you can still end up with one way of seeing things. This is good in the beginning, but as a student advances, it is important for him to develop an insatiable appetite for the subject, so that when he starts to find his voice, he will feel free to evolve without mental constraints.

CHAPTER ᐊ014ᐊ

THE IMPORTANCE OF ART HISTORY

Secrets and Hidden Legacies of the Past

"I have given thee words of vision and wisdom more secret than hidden myster-ies. Ponder them in the silence of thy soul, and then in freedom do thy will."
-Bhagavad-Gita

It is no myth that how much we gain in learning depends on the time we invest. It should please all students of any age or gender to know that no one is cursed or blessed regarding talent. Almost everyone has what it takes to achieve a considerable dream. The student gains according to the time invested and by recognizing his own strengths and talents and capitalizing on them. What prevents an artist from being unique and from having a specific talent that no one else has is only the desire to work like someone else, to make replicas of another artist's work. It is that which gets in the way of an artist finding himself. In my entire teaching career, I have never seen any student who had a specific and unique style that I didn't admire.

It is easier to envision what is possible if you know what has been done in the past and how it was done. Only in art history books can the student find answers, theories, reasons and philosophies that will help him with his desire to become a good artist. The legacies within the pages of books on art can assist the ambitious artist.

If the art student decides to be a full-time painter, chances are he will have to make an extra effort to engage in finding knowledge everywhere. It is part of the artist's natural and therapeutic desire to want to spend most of his time producing physical artworks; often the temperament that leads him to desire to be in the practical field of painting, busily creating, does not include the wish to

Figure 79 -80 JOAQUIN BATISDA y SOROLLA, *Hispanic Society of America*
For posters of Joaquin Sorolla's work, call (212) 926-2234 or visit: www.hispanicsociety.org

sit for hours and hours reading in search of knowledge.

It is for this reason that most art historians cannot paint as well as their artist peers. Most painters do not find the time to read all there is to read about art, which is why good painters do not have the scholarly skills to defend their work like art historians. Reading and learning about art history takes time away from creating. In order to be good enough to create beautiful quality art the artist needs time. But it is important for the serious artist to study the history of art, to learn about the past achievers who have left us with so many important legacies that can better our understanding of the artist's journey.

The student will have to use some of his leisure time to learn as much theory as possible. He will have to educate himself through the intensive study of art history. What the student learned in school are ideas that often support a

particular point of view that is often not broad enough for the student's own
development. I learned all that I know about art theory not from school but by
taking the subway three hours a day seven days a week for fifteen years reading. Three hours stuck on the subway can make you aggravated, or it can cause
you to listen to music or to read, or to duel with your worries. You can even
read romantic books. I chose to do that which suited my art.

All great paintings demand the deepest knowledge,
wisdom and an unfailing craft.

Read, read and read about the history of art. I especially recommend doing so if
the student does not have any previous experience in art history. The student
will have to develop an insatiable appetite for reading everything on art. Also,

Figure 81

For inspiration I purchased this original hand written letter by John Singer Sargent to Richard Watson Gilder, poet and editor of Scribner's Monthly / Century Magazine.

The letter by Sargent translated:

*August 12th
My dear Gilder,
I am sorry to say I have failed in obtaining the consent of owners of recent pictures to have their portraits reproduced. Perhaps Mr. Marquand would not object... (one or two illegible words)... You would like that one - and I am most willing, but in that case I hope another photograph will be taken of it than the only one I have seen which is very poor.
Yours sincerely,
John S Sargent*

the student should strive to develop the joy of knowing more. The student who knows more and pursues a knowledge of art history will understand what has been accomplished and tried in history, what can be built upon in the future, and how the minds worked of the masters who came before us. It is by getting into the minds and ideas of scholars who dedicated all their lives to studying and recording the legacies of the past that the student learns the important reasons that support the artists odyssey. The student with access to this important knowledge and information will be better prepared to pursue the field, more so than those who only know the practical side of art. The knowledge the artist acquires through studying the work of the scholars of all ages contributes to how the artist handles his own artistic adventures. Ideas, movements, problems and situations—faced during learning become familiar rather than strange to the student.

The artist does not paint well just because he has learned to paint well. The learning of technique only makes the artist more technically proficient. History tells us there have been many painters who have been better technicians (more skillful) than some of the great masters, who even produced more than some of

Figure 82

Corner of My
Studio in Union
Square, New York

them, and yet their works have vanished into obscurity. It is the mind and vision behind the talent that separates artists. Art history also tells us that we are just like those who came before us. History too sometimes comforts us during our times of failure. It is only through the study of art history that we too can learn to accept our failures with grace and normality, and handle our successful times with caution, carefulness and humility. Only through the study of art history can we challenge ourselves with realistic dreams, and when things don't go well we can feel we are not the first to fail. Only with art history can we find the realistic humility to succeed. The lives of the masters of the past can help us shape and better our own lives.

Almost all the secrets of the field are hidden within the pages written by various scholars. Any one book does not have all the answers; even if it did, no serious student could afford to ignore the opinions of other scholars. The painter who uses his extra time to find those hidden secrets will have an extra edge.

In a growing culture like ours, it is very difficult to find any successful and ambitious person who doesn't have knowledge about the chosen field she is in. The same goes for scholars. Most experienced art history scholars have had some hands-on experience making art. Once a gallery owner and art dealer told me that she makes her employees take art classes so that they can understand what goes on in the artist's studio in order to better represent her artists. It would also be educational for the artist to work in a gallery in order to understand the gallery owner's side of the story and why his or her goal is to make as much profit as he or she can.

The rewards of reading books, as well as magazine and newspaper articles about art, are so great that no art student should ever spend a week without reading something on art. Read anything related to the arts—modern, classic or experimental art, as well as the philosophy and history of art, anything and everything. Painting alone cannot provide answers to all that we are searching for nor can the creative process alone take the artist to the next higher level in his field. Those who know where they are coming from and where they are, know how to prepare themselves for where they want to go.

Gauguin said, "Often it is history that proves that inspiration is not a myth. What men have done, men can do." It is in the scholarly books that you will learn that you are not alone in your quest to find answers to noble ideas. It is in the history books that you will find out how others discovered solutions to age-old questions. Only in the history books will you find that you're not alone in your thoughts, ideas and goals. Only in the history books will you realize that things have not changed that much. You will learn that the field remains the same but the artists change.

As a student, it is only by knowing how past artists pursued their work that you can determine if you are on the right track or not. Comparing the amount of information the student can get in any book with the book's price, it is advisable for every student to have books as their personal companions. While the hands-on method of teaching and personal contact with teachers is a better way to learn than learning from books, when the student doesn't have access to these things or if the student needs to sharpen some of his skills (not to mention having a convenient reference tool), then books are the best thing.

CHAPTER ◄015◄

CHALLENGES IN THE PURSUIT OF EXCELLENCE

Your Worth as an Artist

In real life, a person's worth might seem to be based on his educational background, his race, his family's name or the religious or political background he comes from. It might even appear to be based on the wealth he has inherited. But the more natural basis for his worth is what he has done, what he knows, what he can do and what his goals and visions and purposes are. These realities of life are the main reasons why we seek education to improve ourselves or our work. We artists, when dreaming, can assume that we are exceptions to these realities, but when we snap out of our dreams we realize that we are creative beings living in a real world. The artist's worth too is based on his mind, knowledge and experience as well as his ideas and visions. If what you know and experience is meaningful to society, society will reward you so you can create more.

Whether the artist or talented individual who is seeking education is motivated by the realities of life, his personal ambitions or by his purpose for living is that individual's personal choice. Education legitimizes you with tradition. For starters, you may be motivated to improve on your talent because you know such development will bring you some sort of freedom and peace.

When talent, discipline and intelligence go together,
repeated success is achieved.

DEVELOPING ARTISTIC TASTE

Good, Mediocre or Amateurish How Do You Know the Difference?

It is inexplicable to me why taste is not thought of as a separate important subject that requires special skills to teach. Whenever one raises the topic, it becomes a philosophical discussion. The art student is on his own when it comes to finding knowledge on the subject. Sometimes he doesn't understand where and how to find out what he needs to know. He cannot distinguish what is corny and cheap from what is classic and timeless. He cannot distinguish among the good, the bad and the bizarre.

Of all the skills that get attention because of their direct effect on students' technical abilities, taste is the most ignored area when it comes to improving skills. The subject of taste is so abstract and illusive that it raises a number of questions and often it is easier just to leave it alone than to try and educate people to understand. For starters, let's begin with a consideration of what one can consider beautiful or how to differentiate between good, bad or ugly in nature. The colors that attract a six-year-old are not the same colors that a six-teen-year-old will like. A twenty-six-year-old will not like the same colors as someone who is forty, and forty is not the same as fifty, nor is fifty the same as sixty-five. The same is true of fashion. These age-related changes of taste are the same in everything. The more we know about a certain subject, the more we can no longer ignore the subtle details that the average uninformed mind doesn't pay attention to. If this is true of clothing, food, music, language and behavior, why not art? After a certain amount of exposure to a certain environment, the artist will wear, eat, speak and think in a certain way in order to best communicate effectively.

What is acceptable before a student gains experience in the field becomes unacceptable when the student knows better. Refusal to accept these realities can affect one's abilities to communicate effectively in any medium. If you are aware of these changes, you can change for the better.

Even though art is individualistic, it is not excluded from the professional fields. Art is a noble profession that is well understood; the artist can communicate well. After all, we create for the people or society we live in. We should have some sense of the various social classes of our times, and how these class-

Figure 83

INDIAN
BRONZE,
Bhagavad Gita

es behave, their likes and dislikes. It would take several pages to give the reasons why one group's taste is better than another's, but that is not the purpose
here. As you improve and develop as an artist, pay attention to the things that
attract you or the images that you gravitate to. Pay attention to the paintings
that you draw inspiration from. Use your student period to improve in every-

thing. The things you select to paint can come across as cheap, tacky and cheesy, as well as natural and classic. It all depends on your taste. Whether an artwork will be dated or timeless and universal depends on the experience and knowledge of the artist. Whether the artist's taste is local, or universal and timeless, what comes out of his creative mind will reflect that taste. Great things appear to have happened by luck. But we know experienced professionals do not rely on luck.

While there is good taste, bad taste, classic taste and cheap taste as well as timeless taste and corny, talking about the various forms of taste is not the purpose of this book. Here I want to describe for you the student who has chosen a noble path. Taste is a topic on its own and needs to be considered more seriously than I can do here. At the very least

Figure 84 SAMUEL ADOQUEI, *The Ballerina, oil on canvas*

it's good to know that you have cultivated your taste and can create for a certain particular segment of your society as you wish and at the same time create whatever you wish. The difference between cheap and tacky artworks and classic universal timeless works lies within the cultivated mind of the artist. Any mind left uncultivated will just feed on the resources previously gathered.

Taste is a necessity in architecture; it is very important for the architect who wants to expand his scope in order to see and study as many buildings as possible. He has to be able to look at buildings dating from thousands of years ago to the modern glass buildings of today. It will be out of these studies that he will shape his own sense of what is beautiful and what is ugly as well as what is good, bad or mediocre. Fine art always has a message to deliver and for this reason there is no good, bad, ugly or mediocre in art. It all depends on whom the artist is communicating to. The well-informed artist with versatile skills is more likely to hit his target. This is commonly seen in politics; the experienced politician communicates according to the taste of his audience. He knows the likes and dislikes of the various classes in society. The artist needs to cultivate his taste so that he will have what it takes to satisfy the needs of those involved when he is confronted with a project in the future.

The argument that beauty is in the eye of the beholder does not hold much ground at the professional level. Standards of quality have changed in the arts because the media, in pursuit of sensational news, have started to extend the foundations art stands on, making room for all that is different. Different and new is now better.

No matter what the reason is, it is in the interest of the student to learn the skills. When he is a student, it is too early for the artist to discriminate.

"Beauty is in nature and occurs in reality under the most varied aspects. As soon as one finds it, it belongs to art, or rather to the artist who can see it."
—Gustave Courbet
Signor Gustave Courbet said this after much experience, when he had become a major figure in the arts.

MY METROPOLITAN MUSEUM EXPERIENCE

(In Pursuit of Excellence)

Years ago, when I first came to the United States. I became so obsessed with the Metropolitan Museum of Art in New York City that I couldn't let a month pass without visiting the museum. For over seven years, I visited the museum several times a week. I visited every Friday and Saturday night and two hours on Sundays. I visited the museum so much that, during the days I couldn't visit, I felt guilty no matter what else I decided to do that weekend.

One day after my visit I picked up my backpack from the checkroom and was getting out of the museum. At the front door, just when I was about to exit, a security guide called me back and asked to search my pack. Normally, security officers at the door do not check on visitors, so I was a bit upset seeing that other visitors were passing by without being checked. I was the only one getting checked.

Although I was now upset I decided to keep my cool. But I lost my cool when they decided to check my bag like immigration officers do. I asked them if they have to go that far. "Yes, we have to," was the reply. Then the guard added, "You know we will get fired if we allow workers from the museum to walk out with their bags unchecked."
"But I don't work here," I said.
"Oh, please, we all know you work here, everyone knows you work here," he continued.
"No," I said, "I am a student."
"Oh, really," he said. "Everyone at the museum thinks you are undercover security. Everyone gets serious about their work when they see you coming around."
"Oh, no," I said. "I am a student and I love coming to visit the museum; it is heaven to me."

For advanced students, no inspiration can surpass that which you get from visiting museums; there you can see the work of all kinds of artists. Some will inspire you, some will motivate you and others will encourage you. Yet others will keep you on your toes, reminding you how far you have come and what you need to do to keep the fire burning.

Even though I was already a professional before my arrival in the U.S., I realized that only at museums could I really see art in person. I had finished school and had done some professional projects, but at the museums, I could see how the Old Masters went about solving their painting problems. If you study long enough, you will every now and then stumble on some secret no one else has discovered and that you alone will understand.

DEVELOPING ARTISTIC TASTE

Developing one's taste doesn't mean one's current taste is bad; rather it simply means the artist should see as many great artworks as possible. He should see so much great art that he can distinguish quality. He can learn to differentiate good and excellent from bad and mediocre. Every now and then, the argument that beauty is in the eye of the beholder can influence an artist into thinking that he need not be influenced too much by great art. That instead, he needs to maintain what he has, not realizing that what he has results from his surroundings and a lifetime accumulation of knowledge. What, after all, is one's personal uniqueness? Or what makes one artist the artist? In Art, the artist's uniqueness is the sum of all the experiences the artist has gone through, as well as what he has gathered from all the paintings he has studied. And also all the books he has read. For a good and sensitive artist, every little thing counts.

Naturally great artists have always been curious beings who travel a lot, read a lot and see a lot. They experiment and always seek growth. They keep searching to find that which will make them better. This is apparent when one studies the chronological changes in the work of all great artists.

In the beginning, when the student is just developing his skills in all the important areas, it is difficult for him to know his own taste in how he sees things and in what attracts him. In such situations, the student will have to rely on art books and prints from museums and from association with mentors or other professional artists. I have always liked developing my universal sensitivities in what I create, for just the reason that I want more people to relate to my

Figure 85 INDIAN ART, *The greatest challenge after school is developing artistic taste in all forms of beauty. Unlike commercial and fashion beauty, timeless beauty does not change. This masterpiece epitomizes the ideal color arrangements in composition. I can never stop looking at this painting without admiration. It takes me everywhere yet bringing me back to the figures, it does not have the western form of center of interest that one expects from Rembrandt yet the message is as strong as any masterpiece of western art . One of the most hypnotic compositions I have ever seen. For inspiration in composition, I have always kept a poster of this image.*

creations than just a selected few. Because my creations are my message, it would have been far easier for me to capitalize on my African roots. But imagining what the world will be like in the future, I decided that if I capitalize on my roots, then my message will reach too small an audience in a world that is becoming smaller and smaller. The vision of great artists, musicians, leaders and politicians is always universal.

With a cultivated taste, the noble artist can touch more people. He can communicate universally, yet the artist will still have his own voice.

CHAPTER ◂O16◂

ART COMPETITIONS

Competing for Awards, Projects or Commissions

Sometime during the student's evolution/career, he might face a situation where he will have to compete for something: scholarships, monetary prizes, awards or project commissions. In a positive sense, competition can also be a way for the student to know where he stands among other artists around the nation; competition helps the artist to assess what he could be lacking, and to understand what others are doing and how others respond to his work. In a positive way, competition helps the artist know what is going on outside his comfort zone. Also, in a respectful way it can create a challenging environment where artists work hard in order to continuously do better. Competition is very good if the student or the artist has good and sincere reasons to compete and maintains the right attitude. As the student graduates or gets ready to move on to the professional world, he may have no idea of the fierce competition awaiting and how he will be forced to compete. It is inevitable that the student will eventually face some rejections as he develops as an artist, and competing is a way to start building up courage (and thick skin) for the future. But this is not the only reason why artists compete.

The desire to compete is often driven by several motives: the need for financial assistance, vanity, professional advancement—sometimes for educational purposes, to test where one stands in the field among other artists. Sometimes artists compete just to win more awards in order to feel good. Competing in order to live, or survive, is natural and helps the artist improve in several ways. To compete for financial assistance is often the best reason to compete. Competitions are designed by institutions to motivate, inspire and encourage artists. Competing psychologically toughens up the advanced student's temperament. In competing, the advanced student puts himself in the hands of jurors for acceptance or rejection. When accepted, the student will have the privilege of seeing his work in the midst of that of other good artists from different backgrounds. Besides these natural and practical realities, I will be the first to warn every student to be careful and cautious with competitions.

Beware of the Competitive Mind

In a way, there is no competition. I will say it again—there is no inherent competition among artists. It is the modern phenomenon of triumphing over your friends that has created another sort of competition. Amateurs, for some reason, need competition so much and believe in it so much that they will create some and search for some where there is none. Artists, by and large, create the competitive environment for themselves. All artists have some natural and special qualities that make them different and unique but when they finish school they don't follow their intuition and focus on their strengths, likes and dislikes. They don't also respond to and improve that which makes them different and unique. They indirectly, and unaware of it, go out of their way to put themselves in a competitive environment. Students try to paint like someone else, and by doing so they create a semi-competition with those they copy,

The only time there is true competition is when there is a commissioned work to be done and the patron is not too sure what artist to choose.

Artists create competition themselves by drawing their inspirations and ideas from the same artistic traditions and philosophy that inspire many of their mates. When several artists develop a very similar style and technique, paint in similar ways and similar subjects, this creates a perfect recipe for competition among groups of artists who believe in the same theories of what art is and what art should be. These are reasons the student should always be careful with addictive styles that might be hard to break away from. The student who develops his skill in an environment that produces look-alikes will face indirect competition with his own friends so that even if he wins, he will still win as a follower of the leader of the group. Some examples are the students of Rembrandt and the followers of Sargent. This scenario forces the art enthusiasts or the collectors of art to discriminate between the originator and visionary of the style or the students and the followers. If this happens the "follower or student of" can get out of this situation and establish his own reputation by using the techniques leaders and politicians have used for centuries. "Being different." Respect and acknowledge all that your father has done for you but don't compete with your father—for all those who help you it is a bad karma. If you do the opposite of what has made your father, he will even help you build your own kingdom. One of the adventures of art is searching for one's own vision

Figure 86

A Painting Studio

In this picture the canvases indicate several art students are painting the same subject. This is a classic example of art students painting the same subject in order to learn to solve technical problems.

through various innovative attempts. This is where the open-minded artist has the natural inherent abilities to do or experiment as he wishes until he finds his vision. He tries and attempts innovative subjects. He attempts innovative compositions and different ideas. And he does these things with the help of his mentors or teachers.

By nature, you inherently have your own taste as well as some traits that make you different from every one else. Explore your differences; your mentor will help you find them. It is to his interest that you too become king or queen of that which you have worked hard to discover. It is good karma for him to teach you in a way that helps you find your own language or path so that both of you grow together. The world is big enough and the history of art broad enough so that there will always be room for unique artists. The advanced student or the intermediate artist should work as hard as he can to avoid beating other artists. In striving to be better than any one else you will loose sight of developing your own unique vision. Save your time and energy for the more important things in an artist's life. Compete ONLY with yourself, your progress.

Figure 87 JAN MANKES, *Aquarium*

The camera creates the third competition for artists. Because most artists never
worked long enough to develop and master their skills, personality and likes
and dislikes while they were students, they end up having to rely on the camera
for everything from imagining an idea to seeing how the final work will look.
They let the camera, a mechanical device, make all the decisions. Nowadays no
one can tell the difference between works by artists from Germany, France,
America or Russia because the work of everyone who is copying from the camera has the same look. The camera and the computer have, indirectly, helped
the sincere artist with an honest eye to have his own space and vision in the art
world. I expressed these reasons in the previous chapters for why the student at
school should avoid employing and relying on the camera and computer. Like I
said before, only when the student has learned to paint well, has developed
strong imaginative talents and has acquired some experience can the camera be

of some help. When everyone's work has the look of the camera, it becomes difficult for individual artists to maintain their uniqueness.

The artist can avoid competing with his friends for galleries by tapping into his own special differences, the personal style he has established and improved on and his unique vision. If within an area there were several delis selling the same thing, it would not be wise for a new deli owner to open a new deli within this same five-block area and sell exactly the same thing as the others. This is very simple logic and might sound like a matter of simple common sense, even insulting advice, to any intelligent person. But, believe it or not, artists have made exactly the same mistake over and over for centuries and are still making it without realizing it. Often advanced students are so oblivious to what the problem is that they don't know how to solve it. In advertising and marketing, the client is always advised to be different and unique to avoid competition. This valuable advice does for an artist too. Whenever an artist achieves a certain successful look or subject matter and becomes popular through his own hard work and personal achievement and through finding his own vision and voice, a flock of other artists, without being aware of what they are doing, move in and copy or emulate his style, idea or technique. Sometimes they even adopt the same subject matter in hopes of achieving the same success. In doing so, they create tough competition for themselves. It is very hard for any artist who has ten to twenty artists painting like him—using the same technique, similar subject matter and with inspirations and ideas coming from the same traditional philosophies—to succeed.

It will be very difficult for any group of people who use the same language, the same accent and who speak about the same things, with inspiration coming from the same place, to stand apart from one another. Such art from a distance might seem inspirational but when one looks deep enough, it is obvious how easy it is for artists to fall into the habit of painting exactly like someone else; they seem to see with the same eyes and mind, they seem to have the same likes and dislikes. This is the major reason competition becomes commonplace. Artists fall into this trap of imitating, often because the inexperienced student does not think far enough ahead, and he dives head first into attractive and popular styles and techniques. One can speak the same language as his community; in languages one does not have to change his natural accent. But he can avoid talking about the same things as everyone else and he can get his inspiration from a different source.

Competition for the sake of vanity and status can be ignored because the energy the student (artist) spends to win can more wisely be spent on improving his own work. Man-made competition is not worth building a career on. The rules of this kind of competition change too often.
Competition is good, but it has its side that can be damaging to the artist's development.

In art, the student can avoid all these self-imposed competitions by just realizing that what works and looks attractive to one artist might not work for everyone. And if the student works hard enough, follows his own calling in an honest way, and relies on nature, he, too, can unveil something unique. All successful styles and techniques, if done well enough, can become classics. This is something I discussed in the chapter on Vision.

"One generation's philosophy is another generation's common sense."
(A proverb from a fortune cookie)

It is not that difficult to find one's own path in the arts. So long as the student can avoid being driven in by the taste and standards set forth by those dealing in the arts, he can succeed as an original. There wouldn't be any competition for artists if they all had their own unique messages. Ten artists with ten unique and different personal messages will be ten different artists. But ten artists using the same technique, producing works with the same look and inspired by the same source would be more than enough for the art enthusiast to sift through and find the One, and crown him. Pissarro and Cézanne came from the same place and sometimes painted side by side. They painted the same subject and yet they are so different in their uniqueness—they differ in terms of technique, style and temperament and they never competed with each other. The same goes for Van Gogh and Gauguin, Sargent and Sorolla, Picasso and Matisse. If they had any sort of competition, it was a positive one, for growth. A creative competition, a pleasant competition that brings out the best of everyone, is very healthy. When I was at art college a friend of mine and I used to compete to see who can draw more figures during our time off from school; sometimes we competed to see who will have the guts to stand and draw in the most congested, crowded area, like the center of a very crowded marketplace. We competed to see who would stand there longer. We also competed to see who could paint longer without food. We made up the competition as we went along; the winner had to take his friends painting. There were other challenges but I don't want to give you, the reader, bad ideas. In a positive competition, everyone wins. On the educational level this happens in studios and on the professional level it often happens between friends who feed on each other's talent but strictly in a positive manner. The caution in this situation is to choose your artistic friends wisely to avoid others copying your ideas. Good friends are supportive of each other and believe there is an abundance of art enthusiasts for everyone. They understand each other and help and support each other.

If the student wants his work to look like that of several artists living in the same place then that is the student's own prerogative. If not, the student should quickly acknowledge the skills he has learned, then use that knowledge to do things that feel natural rather than copy the current trends. Most often, when an artist gets anxious trying to do better than another artist, this forces him to join the professional world to compete. In this anxious competition, he ends up doing the same as the others around him. Yet if the same energy had been spent doing something natural, the artist would have paved his own path without competition.

The new professional should constantly be encouraged to do something he likes. He should develop so much respect and love for his peers, that instead of competing with them, he will be inspired and motivated by them.

The higher the artist raises his bar of ambition, the more he will develop his own natural taste and keep his own voice. Then, without any effort, he will be good, different and unique.

Whether competition is good or healthy for a student, depends on the kind of mind the student has while competing. If approached with the right attitude, competition is very good and healthy for the student or the artist. It motivates, challenges and feeds the desire to keep doing better and growing. On the other hand, when the mind of the competitor is governed by vanity and ego, competitions can be very damaging to the development and improvement of the artist. Competitions do not make or break artists, they only help. The taste of collectors varies so much. Winning in art competitions is not about winner takes all and neither it is like the Oscars where an artist wins an award and with the award comes millions and millions of dollars. There is always some collector who will like an artist's unique way of seeing and portraying the world around him, and this collector won't have been persuaded by competitions.

If for some reason, several clients respond to one particular artist's work, it is not because that artist is better than other artists, it is only because he has developed a certain vision or message that suits the taste and temperament of the group that likes his works and it should inspire you too to develop your work so that you can find your own group of collectors. The energy it takes to win over other artists can be used to find one's own strength and vision. Trying to win awards can only make the artist a chaser of awards and the artist will only pick up leftovers. Most artists aware of this situation find out that it is much easier to develop and improve one's own strength.

Very early on, just after school, the student can spend a year or two exploring his ideas regarding subject matter to see how people respond. The student who copies or follows others will be slowly assassinating his own character, reputation and personality. Each artist arrives at a certain style because his personality, character, temperament and background forced him to gravitate to that style; therefore the same style will not be good for a different artist.

Competition shifts the focus or desire to grow and create great things to just winning for the sake of feeling like a winner. As I have indicated in the section on awards, there is a trick to winning and those who learn the trick go on to win many competitions and awards. Every now and then, some prizes are worth competing for, but most competitions aren't worth the sacrifice.

When accepted into a competition, it is a very good experience for a student to see his work hanging among a variety of artworks, and if the student is honest enough with himself, he can assess where he stands among the artists he is showing with, which will then help the student to go back to the drawing board, continue working hard and come back better prepared.

In any case, it is best for the student to look at competition as a necessary human behavior and accept it as a rite of passage into the professional art world. The results of any competition can't break, or shouldn't break, any artist because behind the scenes of any competition there are sometimes inexplicable reasons why decisions are made. Most of these decisions are made to help the artist indirectly. For these important reasons, it is best that the artist just respects the organization's decision and keeps trying. The organization in general has done more good for artists than artists have done for the organization.

All in all, it is worth the experience to accept competition as part of the artist's evolutional stages and to try to have a positive attitude towards competing; it can be a very good educational experience.

Figure 88 CIDNY KLEIN

The picture I have painted of competition so far is not all that pretty. I did this only because one of the purposes of this book is to bring the realistic side of the competition experience to your awareness to help balance the idea that becoming an artist has only a romantic side. There is also a reality side to learning and developing and toughening up in order to become a serious artist. The more aware you are of both sides, the more fun you will have in participating, and your experiences in competing will not be taken too seriously. Experiences in competing will be part of the learning process. Competition is fun, exciting and important, but most of all it is reality. To fully enjoy the process, the student should understand and accept the whole package; this will mentally prepare the student. If he does not, it can become a bit of a disappointment.

The process of competing is very rewarding; you submit artworks and then you get accepted. You frame the piece, take it to be hung for the exhibition, your friends come to the opening to support you, drink some wine and eat some cheese. If you are lucky, you win an award and life is good; if not, it is just another experience. If you are ambitious, you can capitalize on the whole process and the rewarding feelings and be inspired and motivated to work harder. If you miss getting into one exhibition, so be it; it is not the end of the world, the experience will not define who you are. Never let it upset you to the point that the experience of competing becomes discouraging.

How to Jury Art Students' Work: Awards and Prizes

There are several effective ways for the new student to choose an instructor, but his awards and prizes are not what a student should base his decision on. Do not judge artists by the awards in their portfolio. There is a strategy for winning awards and those who master that strategy go on to win awards. The strategy most artists apply is to take an impressive photograph and work until their painting of it becomes like the original photo but in a painting form. Or they set up some amazing subject matter and work hard on it until the artist gets it right regardless of the time involved. In essence: the strategy is to spend all of their energy on one minor "presentation" of their art that attracts attention and wins over judges. It is a very good strategy for professionals who know what they are doing but not good for students who should be learning. In most respectable institutions, the process of judging is fair and encouraging, which is why these institutions do well and influence so many painters—they always chose fairly.

But in some institutions, the jury gets personal; it is as if the jury makes decisions motivated by their self-interest, not for the well being of the student and the institution. Often juries don't take into consideration who they are judging, whether students, professionals or in-betweens. This creates a discouraging environment. Decisions made by jurors often discourage more students than they inspire and encourage. A jury in pursuit of making a personal statement forgets what yields the best result for the whole institution. In some schools, the jury can be so small-minded that one wonders if the jury is aware of the real purpose of the award. And how sabotaging it is for a school to reward an undeserving student? Fortunately, this doesn't happen that often in professional organizations where too much unfairness can backfire and change an image of a reputable organization. Good organizations build on their reputation for fairness and often the selections of artists and the awarding of prizes alone can tell what the institution is about.

I am from the tradition where an institution awards students according to

Figure 89

JAN GOSSAERT,
Mary Magdalen,
circa 1525-30,
oil on panel

49.53 x 39.37cm
(19 ½ x 15 ½ in.)
Museum of Fine Arts,
Boston, Gift of
William A.
Coolidge,1991

their talent and effort and eagerness to learn. The good, hardworking student struggling to create inspiring artworks is accordingly acknowledged. As in other professional environments where the image of the institution is at stake, awards are given to encourage and influence success through hard work. Awards are given to encourage new students to look up to experienced students as examples; new students hope that if they too work hard enough, they might one day win something. Awards are a way of telling the winners that, "We know you have been working hard, we acknowledge and encourage your effort to produce good work." Awards also say, "We are also aware that you put in lots of energy and time to create the work we have selected. Keep it up, continue working with this focus." It is on this kind of work ethic that most great artists have built their reputations.

With the symbolic gesture of the award, the school is indirectly encouraging the winner to inspire the aspiring students. Awards tell the students that the chance of success increases with such ethic. The school is about learning and hard work. The school, in a quiet way, is reminding the students of the real world. In the real world you will compete and the effort and focus you demonstrate, with your ethical qualities, is promising. If you keep it up, you will have a bright future.

But in the era of "anything goes," a juror who tries to make a statement or disregard the intent of the award thereby fails to consider the influence that awards have on the learning environment. In satisfying his personal partiality through the award, the juror ends up making it harder for the hard-working student to find encouragement. The juror who does not know how awards affect the student, his classmates and the school, ends up sending mixed signals to the winner who does not deserve winning. I have seen total beginners enrolled in art school win the most prestigious awards because their work looks different to a jury that is trying to demonstrate some theory and is careless about how their careless or selfish decision impacts the positive environment of the school and ultimately destroys the work ethic and morale of students. An honest, well-deserving award creates an environment of constant positive competition among the students and in the end everyone wins, including the school.

The student who wants to win should only do so by focusing on acquiring the best education. Other than that, the student, after he's completed school, will learn the hard way. He will learn that in the real world, collectors and buyers of art and art enthusiasts respond to art differently than jurors do. While a juror might pick an artwork because of its credentials, a collector might collect a work because of what it stands for. The exhibition juries will not be the people with galleries, and they will not be those who will provide income so the student can keep working and afford life's necessities. In the real world, galleries only worry about their business. Galleries know what goes on in schools as far as awards and prizes go, and how they are often awarded unfairly. Galleries don't always have respect for awards—their primary concern is more like, "Show me what you can do and how well you can create an artwork." These are the realities outside school.

On the other hand, the most encouraging, inspiring acknowledgement for a hardworking student, who continues his effort to improve while learning and devotes more extra time than the average student, is a well deserved award. An award that goes to the deserving, hardworking student helps everyone; it motivates the student and his aspiring classmates, and it indirectly helps the school too. A deserving winner creates a positive competitive environment, which helps to cultivate promising talents. This motivates the aspiring student.

Because of my professional and teaching awareness, I judge art shows based on whether the show is for professional artists or students. In most situations, my formula for judging and awarding artworks is based on the following qualities: the artist's talent, skills and potential. Devoted, dedicated, talented and hardworking students always display these three qualities. The freedom and evolution of an artist depends on these three elements. With these qualities, the artist has control over his vision and destiny. Most of all, he has the freedom to solve technical problems. Over all, entering into any sort of competition or applying for any award or prize worth the challenge prepares the student for the professional world. It indirectly toughens the student up. It helps the student to see his work in the midst of others' work. Whether the judgments are fair or not, the student shouldn't let any sort of judgment discourage him, competitions in general have done more good to good artists and helped produce and encourage great talents.

IN PURSUIT OF EXCELLENCE

Once you become an advanced student and then graduate, you will have to provide for yourself all that you need for your further growth and progress. It is at this stage of the artist's life that students either remain forever stagnant and mediocre or make the leap to greatness with their own following. It is also at this stage that the enthusiasm to do better can lead the advanced student to search and search for whatever will bring them inspiration, motivation and strength to work while they continue learning.

When the advanced student faces this dilemma, one simple exercise I recommend is to start to look for the best in all painters. Especially in the Old Masters, both classic and modern. He should make the effort to find out why a particular artist has gained greatness over time. He should make the effort to see and study artworks without any preconceived notions. The advanced student should develop the habit of respect. He should realize that almost all the masters of the past have something to offer, and it is the duty of the student in pursuit of growth and inspiration to search for that which makes these Old Masters great. What do they offer? Is it their mind, skill, subject, vision, ideas, style or character? Or perhaps some other contributions to the arts. This scholarly approach to studying artworks will seem paradoxical after the earlier discussion when I said that students should first learn the manner of solving technical problems. And avoid mixing up too many different techniques. It is not paradoxical. The difference is between the beginner and the advanced student. The advanced student, ready to graduate, will not have difficulties in studying the masters in a scholarly manner. It is the beginner who has to follow the recommendations of whoever he is studying under. The advanced student can afford to explore because he has already learned the basics. He will only grow after graduation if he cultivates his innate desire and enthusiasm to learn from the best of the past and to allow his discrimination to come from practical and personal analytical study of important artists. The idea is that all great artists were curious about the other artists who lived before them and during their own times. It therefore makes sense that during the search for knowledge, wisdom and inspiration, the artist cannot afford to discriminate. Discrimination without prior and thorough knowledge of any artist is incompatible with the success and progress of an artist.

In the beginning, it is not easy to stop having likes and dislikes. A simple approach to learning to overcome your prejudices and to learning to accept other artists is to take five to seven artists whose work you don't like, then study what makes them who they are. But study with an explorative mind, a scholarly mind and a curious mind, and make it a point to discover some new things you never knew before about them, and see if you get your new discoveries to allow you to view things differently. Often artists judge other artists for qualities that they personally dislike, and thereby lose sight of aspects of the artist's talent that could be helpful to their growth. The travels of Albrecht Dürer and Van Dyke and the art collecting of Dégas and Rembrandt offer insights into the curious minds of these artists and teach us something about how the masters achieved their greatness. It is not the artworks alone we need to study. We miss the point by not realizing that the artworks are the byproducts of the artist's whole life experiences; and it is the manner in which they achieved their greatness that is worth studying. It is this lifestyle that produced the art that those who want to improve can emulate. It is that certain way that they went about doing things—that is what to look for, not necessarily the results.

The Advancing Student (Going the Extra Mile)

At any given moment, either one has a raw talent and needs to improve on that raw talent or one has an educated talent and needs to improve on that. This leaves the freedom to grow solely to the individual. Whether his existing experience and knowledge is the beginning of his artistic journey or not is left for the individual to decide. Whether the artist is satisfied that his existing skills are enough is a different story, but if the artist decides to pursue progress, then the legacies of the Old Masters will be the main place to start.

In order to improve beyond what he has learned so far, the advanced student has to have the desire to continue learning what he doesn't know and what he needs to know in order to take his educational experience to a higher level. Some awareness of these things makes it much easier to focus on gaining new self-knowledge. What kind of experience and knowledge does one need to learn? Without knowing the important things to learn, it is easy for the advanced student to wander around.

Art is a progressive field; there is no end to its growth and creativity. As in life, the artist grows with time; he experiences new things, gets new ideas and has to adapt to nature's ever-changing cycle. Because of this progression, it is inevitable that the open-minded artist will evolve. As an artist's evolution is part of everything he does, this makes art the most interesting and exciting of fields, even at ninety the artist will still be evolving. In the beginning, the student might think the entire world is confined within the school he attends, the studio's environment or the city in which he lives, but the advanced student will realize that growth and development actually start when he graduates and goes out to start searching for his own clues that he can add to the sum of what school has given him.

Without proper mentoring or the right challenges, an advanced student can get stagnant. He can outgrow school challenges, which can become too familiar. His environment can become too familiar too, and the exercises he does can become overly familiar as well. In this situation, whether the student desires growth or not, the right motivation will not be there for him so long as he keeps searching within the school's environment. To escape this, the student has to have the desire, appetite, drive and enthusiasm to know what he needs, and how to find it with the help of a more experienced artist, mentor or teacher.

We know from the legacies of past artists that they too went down this same path, dreamt the same dreams and pursued the same things that all ambitious artists do. We know from history books that they found their answers the same way, by enlisting their curious, questioning nature. They studied how nature reveals her secrets. We also know the traits of the masters include inquisitiveness toward their own past art history. And we know through their journals how they went about their work. Setting up high standards for themselves, they explored the world around them. To the average master, good was never good enough. The joy of progress was in the constant search for those hidden treasures of nature. To the Old Masters it was not what the public said they were that made them, but their own sensitivity, high standards and tradition of innovative approach toward the field as well as the ethical qualities they displayed. Their greatness came from within; so if you dream of achieving greatness, first start cultivating the greatness within—your desire, enthusiasm and need. The artistic field to them was a noble field; therefore, they approached art with all their heart, soul and mind, with everything they were made of and with everything they had access to. That is how they develop their noble vision.

CHAPTER 17

THE ART DEALER'S WORLD

Galleries and the Road to the Professional World
Understanding the Art World

Often the artist's creative mind or creative spirit leads him to not being able to be logical or practical about the business side of the creative field. Because he is living in the creative world and thinking creatively, he sees the world from a creative point of view and misses out on why things are the way they are from the businessman's point of view.

The artist forgets that if the car dealer, the restaurant owner and the deli owner are in business to provide a commodity in order to make profit, so also the art dealer is in business to fulfill the needs of art enthusiasts and make a profit. The reason artists get frustrated with art dealers is through lack of understanding the purpose of the dealer and how the dealer's world functions. Artists make art for creative reasons, and art dealers deal in art for the purpose of making a profit. Every action on the dealer's part is motivated by these reasons: staying in business, dealing in art and making a profit. Until we understand and respect the motives of the dealer, we will always have a hard time working with art dealers and gallery owners as well as auction houses and individual artists' representatives.

Art dealers have to use whatever skills they have for promotion, marketing, advertising, hype, spinning, whatever it takes. Their goals are to stay in business, sell art and make a profit.

At the top of the ladder in the art dealer's world are the auction houses. They are the movers and shakers of the art world. They determine which gallery artists get auctioned. Behind the auction houses come the galleries. The

Figure 90 SAMUEL ADOQUEI, *An ideal framed painting for galleries, oil on canvas*

galleries determine whose work they will show to the collectors. To the gallery
owner, the artist is literally a creative worker who has to produce creative
works of art that should be sellable and profitable. Galleries do not exist to promote artists or make them famous. They are there to work with the artist to
help sell their products, the artworks. It is the duty of the dealer to promote the
works he thinks will sell. Then come the collectors. The collectors only see
what the galleries and auction houses show them. Last is the educational world.
The educational world deals only with educating and producing painters, not
dealing in art and promoting students or artists. The first three worlds are connected; artworks and artists get moved from one world to another world
depending on the galleries and auctions.

   The control of these three worlds is outside the artist. The educational
world is disconnected from the dealer's world. What goes on in the educational
world never gets noticed in the world of collectors and galleries and auction
houses, but what goes on in the auction houses and gallery world affects the
educational world, both directly and indirectly. Any artist who understands and

respects the business side of dealers will do well creating for galleries. It is a professional mindset that most creative people have difficulty in understanding and accepting. But once understood everything becomes logical and things do not seem so cynical.

There are about three ways of getting into these three important worlds.

First, the traditional way:

The student should have a good art education that will prepare him to have what it takes to create artworks to attract galleries. After he finishes school, the student should be able to know what kind of work is suitable for galleries and be able to differentiate between commercial work, creative work and innovative work. This does not mean that only commercial works sells or that creative and innovative works don't sell. All good art can be sold. That is, all art works created with honest and sincere effort by a good artist harbor the possibility of being sold. When I say commercial work, it only means that the artist (student) should consider the needs of the gallery and its clientele when creating for that particular gallery. Galleries cater to a certain clientele and a practical attitude and approach makes it easier and more practical for the gallery to satisfy the needs of their clientele. A gallery that specializes in landscape will not do well with portraits. And a gallery that deals in portraits will not do well with still lifes.

If a student is interested in being represented by a gallery, he should first think about what the gallery might want. This is why I always advise students never to walk into a gallery with your portfolio without doing previous research on the gallery.

Once accepted, then the gallery will introduce the artist to collectors, and the collectors in return will deal with his work at the auction houses. In order to sell an artist's work, the auction house will have to make up a news release in the artist's name. Then the media will pick up the news and announce it to the public.

Second, the modern way:

An artist can keep making noise and shocking news everywhere in whatever way, so that eventually some gallery owner will listen and will take the artist into the gallery world, hoping that someone will invest in this creative, attention-hungry artist.

Third, the ethical and more realistic way:

An artist can *continue building a strong reputation while producing great works that focus on rare subjects.* This work will touch everyone who sees it for the first time. An artist should be out there showing these effective works. Someone will by all means respond.

The easiest way to get noticed is to combine all the strategies explained above—an artist has the power to connect all four worlds: galleries, auction houses, collectors and school.

Even though the student needs to be aware of these worlds, of their existence and importance to the artist, the student shouldn't forget that all the hype is made in the name of business. The student should not be concerned too much about the unrealistic nature of "who's who" in these worlds. It is important that the student should learn that what works in the business world might not work in the educational world.

While still a student, the artist should try to know the difference between the artworks that do well in the business world and the works that do well in the educational world. What does well in an educational environment does not necessarily do well in the art dealers' world.

If the artist imagines he is not getting a fair shake that is not a reason to be resentful towards the art world. Dealers happen to be business people dealing in art. We should embrace their contribution to society. If they don't want what we have, it is because they cannot sell what we have. It is left to us to decide if we want to provide them with what they can represent. Dealers in all fields know that in business it is easier to provide what the market wants than to educate the market to consume what you have. They all know that the graveyard of success is full of great talents and smart businesses with amazing unwanted products.

It is because of the business world that art has been preserved for us. The business world has encouraged and created opportunities for artists. Without the business world, who knows what would have happened. No matter what we think, it is better for the business world to make decisions than for any other group. The business world wants to make enormous profits so it is in their interest that the artist lives and paints. They are not as cynical or personal as we like to think. They are artists in their own right. Therefore, the artist should never resent them, but rather understand their reasons and find his own way to work with them.

It is very important to concentrate on appropriate studio studies during the student periods in order to have some works ready for these business people. If you are good enough and prepared enough, some way along the road someone will be willing to give you a chance. As new artists come on the scene so do new dealers. New dealers are always willing to find opportunities for the new artist. The businessman is an artist in his own right; he creates profits.

An artist can be popular in the professional world and yet unable to teach a class or keep students in any art institution. The same goes for someone who has won a great deal of awards in the art world. That person can walk into a gallery and be surprised that no one has ever heard of him in the gallery world. The professional world, run by the media and the galleries, and the educational world, run by studios, art institutions, art organizations and workshops, do not have the same functions and are not governed by the same laws. Art, for some reason, is like a religion. The art student gets so consumed by his surroundings and so absorbed in his work that he often forgets about the other existing art worlds that live beyond his studio doors. Like religion, "them against us" is always in play; we are doing the right things and they are learning the wrong way. That's why the student is more likely to think the whole world revolves around his small studio.

The student should focus and concentrate on working in a progressive environment and should develop his common sense about the practical world. The student should learn to be aware of the dynamics of the art dealer's world so that he does not develop one-sided taste and narrow beliefs and temperament. It is for the artist's own sake that he should remain aware of what is happening in the art dealer's world. For the sake of survival. It is inherent in all artists to want to end up in the professional world where only the heavy contenders exist, but due to the student's misleading information he often ends up with less than he bargained for.

My advice to students: Do the right thing at school, acquire some working experience, search for knowledge wherever you can get it in order to gain some natural wisdom, then prepare, plan and execute your plan. Sensible artists with experience and a logical approach to their careers can't fail if they follow this way. The Cosmic Law never fails artists with a realistic and honest plan and a good attitude.

Any quick-fix way of getting into one of these three art worlds is possible, but staying in these worlds will require basic artistic strength, with all the parts of the anatomy of a good artist working harmoniously.

The main message in this chapter is to inform the student, the soon-to-become-an-artist, that art dealers are in the professional business. Some rejections we must face as we mature. It's got nothing to do with our work. What we term rejection, actually means; "Dear artist, my gallery doesn't have buyers for the kind of work you do." This is what rejection means.

We should work very hard on ourselves to understand the business aspect of art and not to let rejection affect us. I have had more rejections than anyone I know, but I don't think any of those rejections were meant to be personal or were directed at me. It was only because it was not going to be easy for those galleries to sell my work. With hindsight, it is those rejections that brought me to where I am. There are thousands of galleries out there. If being represented is your goal, then you will surely find one that will be good for you.

How People Buy and Who Buys What

In some research I conducted a couple of years ago, I realized that there are three types of buyers (collectors) of art: the buyer who works and lives on his income, the buyer buying for someone else with unlimited funds (such as a company), and the buyer (often more creative) who is concerned with what everyone else will think. Decisions are often made under the influence of passion. The backgrounds of all these buyers determine how they bargain, what they buy and what they expect from the work as well as which artists they buy and where they buy.

The buyer who uses money earned with his own sweat is very discriminating and often more interested in the artist's skill, creativity and vision.

What art enthusiasts like and what they are willing to spend their money on can sometimes be two different things. An art lover might like an artwork yet he will not be willing to spend his own money on it even if he can afford the

Figure 91 MOISEY KOGAN, *Blue Russia*

work. A good, beautiful artwork might sell eventually but it will not necessarily sell instantly to any potential buyer who sees the work. Recently, I made a survey regarding a class exhibition. I asked students first to choose five of their favorite paintings out of about sixty works. After they had chosen the five, I asked them to choose the two best paintings out of the five. Then I asked them to imagine spending a month's income on one out of their five favorites. The result was that almost two-thirds of the students would have chosen to spend their monthly income on a work other than the two best works that they had chosen.

Next I asked them for the reasons why they chose their two best works. The reasons they gave were all related to their heart's demands—their feelings, strong views, ideas about innovation and other spiritual, abstract or inexplicable emotional reasons. Then I asked them why they would spend their month's income on a certain artwork that they had not included in their best two, and the reasons they gave were mainly driven by what they like and what they can live with and by other logical reasons.

On a different day, I asked the students to imagine being given an unlimited amount of money to acquire two pieces of artwork from the five they originally chose. Again, what they chose to collect with someone else's money was very different with what they would choose using their own money. It became very clear and revealing to me what influences buyers and what should influence the effort we put into creating (and selling) artwork. I experienced the same thing while in India where I was collecting some artwork. All the works that were exceptional were the works I didn't bargain for. I was afraid the dealers wouldn't want to sell if I bargained too much. Yet those works where I thought little went into their creation, I haggled and haggled for until my guide called me on it. It became educational to me regarding how to create and price my work. I wish I had had this knowledge fifteen years ago. I would have tailored my career differently.

I was once teaching a class of mainly advanced artists and conducted a different survey. The subjects they were painting—figure and still life—were set up for a two-week session. At the end of the two weeks, when I had done all my teaching on those particular subjects and the students had finished and had put in their best effort, I went to students individually, and asked them, "Suppose a buyer were to come in and say he is willing to pay five times more for a painting if the artist is willing to spend more time on the work."

I asked each student to consider this scenario and then asked each one what aspects of the painting he would work on; I asked them to write down the list of those things. Everyone listed about seven to twelve things ranging from editing things out to adjusting the composition, to fixing the drawing, background or color. Afterward, I made my point to the students that the average student does not think of what art lovers demand from him. That's why the average artist often doesn't put in his best effort when creating. Students nowadays think, incorrectly, that art enthusiasts and collectors alike do not demand exceptional performance, so why work too hard if "anything goes," and the dealers decide who will be the next Picasso?

Most successful professional creative artists are influenced by the knowledge of how people buy, why people buy and who buys what. This knowledge governs the way professionals work—what they paint, how they paint and how much time they put into the works they do and also the price they demand for their work.

It is true that with a good rap a professional experienced dealer can sell almost anything, but the art student should not rely on what the professional dealer can do. Rather he should put in his best work so he will be well prepared for the professional dealer and for himself when dealing with collectors. When I started my profession a good friend once told me, "All good sensitive works will always sell."

GALLERIES

Your Portfolio and What Should Represent You

Summarized

Five steps to getting into a gallery and how to deal with a gallery: The student should understand the reality of galleries—they are in the business of selling paintings. Therefore, the first step if you would like to get into a gallery is to create good marketable paintings so that the gallery you apply to will profit by investing in your work. Study what a particular gallery wants and create your portfolio with that in mind.

Your portfolio has four purposes. A good portfolio is the way to secure the artist's reputation. It should:
Demonstrate your mastery–what the artist has done and can do.
Demonstrate your preferences and vision regarding subject matter.
Be focused and consistent (don't show nudes, then when accepted bring in paintings of apples). Also, be sure that you focus on a subject or theme that will be an addition to what the gallery you have targeted already shows and that avoids competition with the work of the artists the gallery already represents. Attract attention (the works in your portfolio should attract attention and have potential. They should demonstrate a unique vision).

When preparing his portfolio, the student cannot afford to work without research. He needs to have a couple of galleries or clients in mind while creating (or selecting) works for the portfolio—the kind of works that fit these galleries' tastes. Too many times art students walk into galleries with their student works—works made without any consideration of the gallery or its clients. Even if the artist is lucky enough to be accepted by the gallery, chances are he will still have to go back and create special works for the gallery—works that

Figure 92

JOHN SINGER
SARGENT
(1856-1925),
*Peter Augustus Jay,
1880, oil on canvas*
Courtesy of Adelson
Galleries, New York

can be sold. The ideal situation is to be accepted by a gallery for artworks the artist himself likes and has always painted, but this happens rarely and usually only when the artist does not have to rely on anyone financially for survival.

The more research about galleries the artist does, the more prepared he will be. As a rule of thumb, never send a portfolio to any gallery unless you have been studying its taste (as demonstrated by its exhibitions and the artists on its roster) for at least a year and a half or more, sometimes five years. Never send a portfolio to a client if you have no clue as to what they might like and what they are looking for. Even though you might get lucky, it is easier, more cost effective and more time saving to do research on a gallery or client before approaching them.

Based on the galleries you have studied, make sure the works you have in your portfolio are the best you can do, and use your teacher or an honest peer or mentor to help you choose the selections you will be sending, because as students we are not mature and professional enough to always judge what is our best work. We normally get too personal about our work. That is, we are not objective enough when selecting. Make sure to select seven or ten from more than 20 works. Arrange and present them well in your portfolio before approaching clients or galleries.

Second, create a clientele and a following so that the gallery you apply to would like to represent you in order to have some of your business.

Third, get into a gallery through a reputable recommendation.

Figure 93 SAMUEL ADOQUEI, *Shelter Island*

CHAPTER ◄18◄

THE ADVANCED STUDENT
IN SEARCH OF GROWTH

The Five Immortal Laws of Success for Art Students

Seek skill, experience, knowledge and wisdom, so that you can understand how to create more effective art works. Focus on a style of working that seems very natural to you and explore it.
Cultivate your attitude so that in the beginning your superiors will feel comfortable sharing their knowledge, wisdom, experience and ideas with you.

Know what you desire to create, what feeds you and becomes the fuel for your growth. Create more of the art works that most of society wants, be it a certain subject or a certain style. Use one-third of your time to create what society will benefit from, another third to paint what your heart desires and the last third to seek more knowledge and wisdom. You might desire to paint landscapes but collectors may like collecting your still lifes. Don't fight against it.

Understand and know the reasons why there are all sorts of art; focus on your own art. To the best of your knowledge, do the best work you can. Be positive about everything, but know yourself. Avoid distractions. You are one human entity; you cannot be everyone. You don't have the machinery to paint in every style, but you have tremendous ability to focus and do that which you choose to do and desire to do better than anyone else.

Cultivate your noble self. The desire to be an artist means there is some sort of noble idea you want to pursue. Cultivate that noble mind of yours, as well as your behavior and your actions so that everyone around you can feel and experience that noble heart of yours. Be a truly noble person in every possible instance, in whatever you are doing, from your artworks to your dealings with the world around you. Our noble duty as artists is to add to society, to improve society in a direct or an indirect way. To achieve that goal, it is important to accept the task of encouraging nobility in your being.

Friends and Inspirations
(Food for Thought)

The kind of friends you choose during your student period can challenge and inspire you, and bring out the best of your talents.

As you mature as a student and become a professional it is important to make friends that you respect and admire. Sometimes they may be friends who have a different style, different beliefs and even different ideas and opinions and philosophies of art. But not necessarily the opposite of what you believe in. You should make sure your friends are good artists in their own right who know their field and are experts at what they do. Maybe you can exchange artwork with them and trade reproductions of the masters that your group respects and that are different. It is important for you to develop different tastes, different styles and ideas from those of your friends. This does not mean you should change your own thinking to match theirs but rather allow yourself to develop your own philosophical views. While in school, you become good at doing the same thing as your friends but once you become a professional with enough secure experience, you might need something refreshing and challenging. You might need something different from your friends' views that will bring inspiration and new philosophical insight. You might need something that is good enough to make you see nature through different eyes.

The friends that you make who are different from you are often the ones who have their own strong opinions. If you are open-minded their opinions can be refreshing and even inspiring. Most masters in the arts practiced this behavior all the time. Van Gogh differed a lot from Gauguin yet he went to the fields with him and they painted together.

Michelangelo owned drawings by Leonardo; Dürer was a friend of Giovanni Bellini's; Dégas collected works by other artists; and Sargent copied El Greco. The list goes on and on, so why not you?

This kind of behavior is more obvious and common with musicians. Musicians will go anywhere in the world in search of new ideas and inspiration.

In the arts, uniqueness is almost like a secret. Most mediocre artists do everything together and bash works that aren't like theirs and therefore they remain closed minded.

A friend who is different from you might sometimes have a fierce argument with you but this is an honest argument. If approached philosophically, this fierce argument might help broaden your horizons. Just try not to waste your time on unnecessary arguments or dishonest arguments. When in doubt, develop a sincere appreciation for the modern masters, from Picasso to the Fauves to Diebenkorn. You can always find someone whose work is different from your own. The same goes for contemporary artists—pay attention to the realistic artists.

Abraham Lincoln could not have been wrong to appoint opponents to his staff. Why should a traditionalist like Dégas buy works by Cezanne? Imagine when the drawings of Leonardo were found in Michelango's possessions.

The professional who has practiced his skills and worked hard enough to gain confidence in his abilities and who has been reading art history for years can gain even more by exploring different ideas and new philosophical ways of reasoning about art and by branching out into new territory. This does not mean that you should change your views, style or technique completely. You can be influenced without changing. Philosophers, musicians, dancers and writers never turn their noses up in the air at those who differ from them. Instead they learn from the differences. Those who love arguing or giving opinions are good as charactors in romantic biographies about artists. In real life, it is not worth the energy to have an argument just for the sake of arguing; such a practice will overwhelm the sensitive artist and sap his energies.

The advanced student should always be very careful in choosing friends to make sure they sincerely encourage him and genuinely want him to grow and he should apply the same principles to what he wants for them.

THE PLAN FOR GUIDANCE

A Plan, then a Mission Statement

Recently, one thing that often appears on artists' résumés is the artist's personal mission statement. This is a statement that clarifies what the artist's intentions are. Even though the statement may not necessarily mean to be a done deal (his goals and vision my be expanded later); it explains the visions and goals he has now, what the artist is about. The statement helps the reader know what the artist's intentions are and writing it helps the artist to psychologically focus on some set goals for his creative journey.

Writing down some of our thoughts to help us clarify our intentions and to remind us of our priorities and purposes is well worth doing. Our priorities may change with time and experience, but the written statement of priorities and goals acts as a reminder of what we feel is first and most important on our list of things we hope to accomplish.

A mission statement is fairly abstract and can easily become all about your beautiful abstract dreams and wishes regarding what you want to achieve. But a plan is a more realistic accounting of what needs to be done to achieve a certain purpose as well as the sequence of how and when, as well as which and what to do. For example, my mission statement as a teacher is to work with my students so as to produce good artists but my plan for how to do so takes into consideration the time available, the exercises assigned and the students' temperaments and sensitivities. It also considers the way this plan is executed and how well I achieve these goals.

If we can have a mission statement when we are professional artists, why not have a mission plan for studying to become artists, something that will help a student focus on his priorities. Having such a plan is a common practice among all successful achievers. It's just common sense to have a plan so that everything is handled according to priorities and all tasks are tackled accordingly. Put first things first in order to save time, so you are not swayed by surprises, and to make sure that every action leads to the goals you set forth.

The plans we make and the goals we set to achieve our aspirations and vision are the most important things to worry about if we intend to get profitable results, especially in a field so abstract as art. How we go about the plans we make as students, pursuing art as a vocation, is what this book is about. The conscious decision to give at least some thought to how you (the student) should plan for your art education is also the most important reason to read the book. No art student is better or more talented than any other, but it is necessary for the student to know his or her strengths and weaknesses so that he or she can be in control and focus on his strengths and goals.

Figure 94 Photograph of Jeanette Christjansen at the National Academy School of Fine Arts

Avoid Suffering from Me-Me-Me Syndrome

For the Sistine Chapel to be possible and successful, Michelangelo had to acknowledge the desires and requirements of the Pope. Leonardo had to design things that were not paintings in order to get his foot in the doors of potential patrons. Sargent is known for working to please his patrons. Recently, I saw a television interview on Charlie Rose. It was about a very successful creative writer, who had written over 28 novels and almost 8 of the books have been turned into movies. Despite all his talent and accomplishments, he said he sometimes had to give in to his editors or movie producers in order to make the books or movies possible. He was humble enough to admit that while he is a talented writer, he is not a professional editor or movie producer. And he admitted this on national TV. Imagine!

These are the stories the contemporary student doesn't take into consideration when he is pursuing art as a vocation because he wants to become the next Jackson Pollock or Andy Warhol. I call this the Me-Me-Me Syndrome: "I am this, I want this, this is my work, I want to be unique and different, I will not compromise."

With this attitude of self-absorption, an artist neglects his ability to be of service to society and disregards the mechanics of society and its art enthusiasts. And in thinking this way, he makes it difficult to work well with dealers and gallery owners. The surprising thing is that most advanced students think this way because of their naiveté. The failure to understand how things work in the art world is the enemy of survival as well as the enemy of freedom to work, create and dream in financial comfort. This Me-Me-Me Syndrome is always based on a romantic uninformed idea of what an artist is supposed to be or how an artist is supposed to act—it is never realistic and it is never the reality of the life of any real and truly successful artist. Collaboration and understanding of the society we live in have never taken anything away from the talent of the great creative artists of the past and I don't see it taking anything away from the talent of any artist today. It is always those with less to give who think that any outside influence or collaboration to satisfy patrons will take away from their own original talent. It is those who have nothing to give who think that this is a way of losing one's self. The student or the artist who will not compromise has to understand that after his education, when he is in pursuit of success, the experienced artist will encounter a number of challenges, such as personally dealing with collectors, dealers, gallery owners, publishers and the public, and he will also encounter criticism from several angles, some honest, some biased. How the artist handles these challenges or situations will determine how easy or difficult the artist will find it to achieve success. It is important for the advanced student to be a bit self-aware regarding his skills in dealing with people under any situation.

The success of an artist depends on the artist knowing himself, his endurance, his budget and his time, where he is and where he wants to go. The earlier the student acknowledges these things, and gets to work on his weak-

Figure 95 GERRY HEYDT, *Red Plate*

nesses, the more he can pursue the field with ease and accomplish his desires, dreams and vision.

When a student makes up his mind to pursue art as a vocation, there are some questions the student should try and find answers for: where to study; where to find a mentor; who to study under; what traditional style will best suit his temperament; how long the prescribed course of study will take; and what he should expect when he finishes studying. Asking these questions can help the student make realistic decisions. The price tag for his artistic search varies from the monetary investment to the years of commitment.

For me, when I decided to leave advertising and commercial art to pursue fine art, I knew that turning back was not an option, so I was forced to ask myself these questions and by trying to find answers, to use the answers to set the pace for my whole artistic career. How I work and how I teach is influenced by these questions and their answers.

In the beginning, these questions can be discouraging, but in reality, they are very simple questions and common to other students in other academic fields; it is just because of the abstract nature of art that artists don't consider them. However, answering these questions will make things feel more rational and help you set up some real goals. The artistic pursuit is not as formal as some other careers.

HOW TO AVOID GOING WRONG?

Excellence and Mediocrity

Excellence and Mediocrity do not have to be different genders, come from different places and go to different schools in order to find themselves. Most often, they studied together, sometimes at the same school under the same instructor. Sometimes, they even worked side by side.

The distinctions between them start to surface after school. How then did Excellence acquire the thoughts he thrives on, the oil that fuels his energy, the inspiration that keeps his spirit wanting to go that extra mile, the talent and toughness for endurance? When and how did Excellence distill the fuel that keeps his insatiable engine running? To whom will he credit his success? What enabled him to maintain his enthusiasm? What was his source of encouragement? How did Mediocrity lose his spirit? Why did he give up on his courage and inspiration? What happened to him along the way, and whose fault was that? Why didn't he seek some guidance?

If they both come from the same place, went to the same school and worked side by side, then whatever caused the differences in their achievements can be traced back to what happened in the educational environment, not before or after.

What happens during a student's education will determine how successful he will be. Mediocrity results from ignoring enlightenment that may arise during the educational period. Mediocrity is the result of a certain approach to studies. What is this certain approach?

If the student is lucky, he will find a good instructor with all the best qualities for teaching and for bringing out the best in students. He will be articulate, skillful, knowledgeable, inspirational and motivational. After school, the student is more likely to adopt some of these attributes, or he will have to make an

Figure 96 JAN MANKES, *Two Young Magpies*

enthusiastic conscious decision to develop these invaluable characteristics that teachers have as well as the desire to keep improving himself, to continue growing. This is where Mediocrity and Excellence differ.

Education by nature gives us the tools and keys needed for growth and improvement. Education is the beginning of our artistic vocation. Schools are not the cause of an individual's lack of growth. During school, everything that education provides (such as teaching, knowledge and skills) is available but after school all the necessary elements needed for improvement and growth are hidden. Teachers will recommend books to read, museums to visit, exhibitions to see and point out to the student what lessons to learn from those books, museums and exhibitions. The teachers will show or recommend paintings that should provide the necessary lessons and inspiration.

After school in pursuit of self-improvement, development and growth, the former student will have to be inquisitive enough to be willing to do more work: the necessary research, to read books, see as many paintings as possible at museums and visit exhibitions. He has to do so in search of the elements that will take him to the next stage in his development! He continues to need lessons, inspiration and motivation. He has to search and search and be smart enough to seize any good useful information or ideas that provide these elements for him. This also will be a way to keep his enthusiasm alive.

For these reasons, finding that which you need after school, and knowing that your growth comes according to how curious you are, guarantees that the graduate who is willing will improve, develop and grow. The student who is not privileged to stay in school until he acquires enough skill and knowledge to become a professional still stands a good chance of becoming proficient and better than he was when he left school. He will just have to work harder on his own; it is important to know that. He will need more of the honest appetite to improve himself and more of the enthusiasm to learn—these are the secrets to growth. The appetite and desire that make us search for all that we need.

The student looking back and making some self-assessments can determine to change his ways and pursue his vocation without difficulties because the creative world is more forgiving than any other field. All it takes is to be enthusiastic, to develop a devoted focus on a vision worth sacrificing for.

The art student has no idea of all the wonderful things he could achieve had he realized earlier that to learn more is to know more, and that knowing more will help him do more things easily and that the more things the artist does the greater the chance that some of the things will hit the bull's eye. All artists, by virtue of being artists, are noble creatures, since nobility is the inherent desire to help improve mankind's life and that is what we strive for. Among our grand ideas, dreams, ambitions, goals and vision is our understanding of the field that we have chosen as the main language we want to use. Considering how big our dreams are, it is worth the sacrifice of several years to learn that language well and to have the right approach to learning. The physical, mental and the spiritual are all one and our strength lies in how strong they are.

You can only be enlightened if you subconsciously want to be enlightened. The student can only improve if the spirit is enlightened and the physical body is willing to go the extra miles needed to learn and improve. All things are possible if one accepts that. It is for the goodness of our being that we improve in whatever we do; when we are good at what we do we can accomplish whatever we wish. Then the world we live in will gain from our creations and in return the universe will favor us as it has done for all men who contribute to mankind.

Epilogue

There used to be a time when one could tell the subtle differences among the arts, for example, the difference between art and craft and skill and talent. One could also differentiate the craftsmen from the real artists and the fake ones, but not anymore. There used to be a time when, before the public would accept you as an artist, you would have to display several attributes, such as talent, skill, knowledge, experience and sensibilities, producing works that come from a true and honest conscience, driven by a dedicated desire to create works of art inspired by years of studying in the field. Your whole system was trained and built to pursue art as a vocation. Not anymore.

In recent years, almost anything is art. This is a good sign of how we have evolved. Art is no longer for the privileged or the young. There used to be a time when the accepted art was created by only a handful of cultures; that barrier no longer exists. The barriers of age, gender, race and culture are no longer issues. We are all artists. Those barriers only become issues when dealers get involved. Almost anyone can create in the manner of any culture or style. An Asian can paint in a Western manner or a Westerner can work in an African style.

Because the field is open and level to all and everyone, to be an artist means anything. You can decide to acquire education or ignore it. The title "artist" means that anyone who calls himself an artist is an artist. This way of viewing art and artists is backfiring. The field is level to all. This leveling has taken everything to the past again. The public knows more and they know what is going on. The public is better educated than ever before; they know the gimmicks and tricks and can distinguish among the self-proclaimed artist, using art to cry for attention; the part-time artist, the craftsman and the real artist. As in the past, the field has started to discriminate within itself among the natural-born artists, the artists, the deceptive artists and those who want to be an artists.

Since art became business, anyone can claim the title of artist without feeling awkward. For some decades now, ever since the media became a major source of how we communicate, one can either just claim the title of artist or one can become an artist.

This is why the talented individual needs education. After almost a hundred years of being told that anything whatever is art, the public has learned well and now the public can discriminate among the arts. The public is better educated than twenty-five years ago. They are more demanding regarding the talents and abilities of artists. The public knows who is who and what is what. The public will demand more effort than just the claim of I call myself an artist therefore I am. Talent, skill, knowledge and experience will all be demanded by the educated public. The public keeps getting smarter, and will be more difficult to please. The more experienced, better-educated and more knowledgeable artist will always stand a better chance of making his vision more acceptable.

There is a lot to learn and much knowledge and wisdom to acquire. The mind of the artist has to be supported by experience, knowledge, wisdom and the innate traits of the will to create. Education provides the impetus to start the artistic vocation some steps ahead of the field. The public places the educated and experienced artist in association with all those who came before him. By their doing so, the student is constantly reminded of what is involved in pursuing art. What is required of an artist is his noble responsibility to improve on the world he inherited, the duty to enhance that which we live with. Education also reminds us that how the artists before us contributed to their world and how we gain from their contribution. By having access to the past through education, the student develops a certain healthy mentality, a mentality that wants to do only helpful things for mankind. What the public sees in us is observed through the way education makes the artist live, work and pursue the world.

I started this book by saying that the art and science of art is like the grammar of language. Everyone needs grammar if he wants to know the language and use it to communicate his thoughts, ideas, visions and reasons. The more knowledge one acquires the easier the communication will be. I'd like to end by reminding the student to plan well in order to get the best education, to work hard to save some years, to let his work ethics be motivated by the dreams he has. Plan well so the years you spend will be worth the effort. Always know that the school or studio you work in is just the beginning stage; your best creations await you somewhere in the future. Gather as much information as possible, be as enthusiastic towards learning and growing, as curious and inquisitive as possible toward the Old Masters. When you graduate, be very

Figure 97 JAN MANKES, *Young Starling*

open-minded toward artists better than you, especially the Old Masters, both classic and modern. Remember discrimination without prior and thorough knowledge of any artist is incompatible with the success and progress of an artist.

Figure 98 AFRICAN SCULPTURE